Get

Inspired!

Get

Inspired!

Releasing

Your

Creative Self

at

Any Age

Roy P. Fairfield

59 John Glenn Drive
Amherst, New York 14228-2197

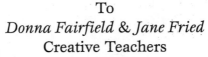

To
Donna Fairfield & Jane Fried
Creative Teachers

Published 2001 by Prometheus Books

Inquiries should be addressed to
Prometheus Books
59 John Glenn Drive
Amherst, New York 14228–2197
VOICE: 716–691–0133, ext. 207
FAX: 716–564–2711
WWW.PROMETHEUSBOOKS.COM

05 04 03 02 01   5 4 3 2 1

Library of Congress Cataloging-in-Publication Data

Fairfield, Roy P.
      Get inspired! : how to release your creative self at any age / Roy P. Fairfield.
          p. cm.
      Includes bibliographical references and index.
      ISBN 1–57392–849–6 (pbk. : alk. paper)
      1. Creative ability. 2. Creative thinking. I. Title.
BF408 .F23 2001
153.3'5—dc21   2001019094

Printed in the United States of America on acid-free paper

Contents

Contents

Contents

Preface

The origin of the word *creativity* and its fundamental concept is caught wholly in the word *originate*. This book is based on my basic belief: that almost everybody, barring serious illness, has a creative vein in their being if they will dig for it, taking advantage of their unique personality, their specific place in the world at a given space-time and motion in that world. My second belief: that while there is a real temptation to judge creations on various scales of "better-than or worse-than," as well as "lower- and higher-than," each person must first look to her or his unique ability to use their five senses and intuition to express their perspectives and insights in the mode suiting them best. After "exploiting" that mode, any person can utilize it, as it seems most appropriate "in the world." But creation will normally precede application although the two processes may evolve together.

While I've written this book during my so-called re-FIRE-ment (as contrasted to re-TIRE-ment) and many applications and illustrations may be aimed at "senior" citizens, I've had sufficient feedback from teachers and other professionals to know that the ideas and suggestions have a wide application for persons of any age in a host of situations.

Such a book could have been long on theory and short on illustrations, but I chose to write for laypersons rather than professors of art history, technology, science, psychology, etc. Hence, it's possible that layfolk may prefer to read from chapter 2 to the end before tackling the introduction. In fact, most chapters can be read independent of one another. This book is also designed to be interactive rather than to be read passively. The exercises, more numerous toward the end of the book, allow for that kind of active dialogue with the absent author—although I've been known to correspond with hundreds of persons who want to engage in dialogue!

Acknowledgments: to Earlene "Kitty" Chadbourne, Deborah C. Goebel, and Robert Reynolds for careful reading of the manuscript, for both mechanical and content suggestions. To Gerry Morin and his staff at the Dyer Library, Saco, Maine, for assistance consistent with technical support, probably more than they'll ever know. To Paul Kurtz for fundamental encouragement to pursue my vision. To many friends and professional associates with whom I have shared and discussed some of my "effusions" over a lifetime of interaction and correspondence, thank you. To Dr. Norman Cohn, a Distinguished Professor at Ohio University and former colleague, for specific help with the concept of the Half-Life of a Question (chapter 5). Also appreciation to those giving me feedback to some of the specific illustrations, which I hope readers may use as do-able models. To editors Steven L. Mitchell and Mary A. Read at Prometheus Books for many clarifications. Also very important, thank you, Maryllyn, for the oceans of patience in seeing this and so many other projects through.

Roy P. Fairfield
Bayberry Point
Biddeford, Maine
Spring 2001

CHAPTER 1

Climate for Creativity

A t 5:30 on a Tuesday morning in January 1949, I dreamed that I was assisting an undertaker friend in putting one of my current, front-row students into a coffin. As we were about to close the coffin lid, the student sat bolt upright and exclaimed, quite characteristically, "You can't do this to me." I awoke my spouse and told her how vivid the dream was. At 11:20 that same morning I related the dream to my student as we entered a lecture hall. He laughed and we went on with the class and the week. The following Saturday night, while walking on the side of a main street, he was killed by an automobile which went out of control during an ice storm.

This traumatic event of precognitive proportions, along with the superstitious climate in which I was reared, helped reinforce my openness to events that defied causal explanations. Also, it led in the direction of a synthesis between the rugged individualism in which I bathed as a Maine boy and speculation about paradigmatic shifts as found in Karl Pribram's holographic view of the universe and discussed widely and wisely by those dealing with "the new physics."[1]

Unique Angles of Vision

In my judgment every society, but especially the contemporary American one, must promote development of unique angles of vision among its citizens. Without our inventors, mathematical geniuses, political and social experimenters—in short, without our dissenters—our courageous spokespersons reflecting "grace under pressure" (Hemingway's definition of courage), without any and every force which honors and/or respects the individual viewpoint, without consistent and persistent questioning of "conventional wisdom," we would run the danger of social, political, technological, scientific, and economic stagnation, to say nothing about psychological lobotomy.

Yet, for all our vaunted rhetoric about valuing dissent, encouraging individuals (we issue them patents and copyrights), protecting the individual's right to speak in the spirit of John Stuart Mill and the American Civil Liberties Union, do we indeed do enough to promote unique angles of vision, perception, action, or thought? In fact, how can we save our country from the wasteland growing from "political correctness" or TV's numbing conformity? While we may find the occasional philosopher-king emerging from our school system and/or Jefferson's "genius raked from the rubbish," do we promote such persons—despite the spate of science fairs, debating clinics, and dean's listings? Only in recent history have we begun to develop school programs and schools for "the gifted." Only recently, at the other end of the learning-potential continuum have we supported human development and mainstreaming of the so-called disadvantaged and/or senior citizens. But what about all of the children/young adults/older folk somewhere in the middle of the learning spectrum, especially in a so-called democratic society and in the context of equality of opportunity?

This is not to condemn what we try to do in this direction nor is it to deny collective approaches to learning and/or human development. Rather it is my intention to suggest ways and means by which we may stimulate even further the hands-on approaches being made by science and children's museums, by any and every institution with the courage to seek its visions amidst incredibly powerful forces to level individual efforts, to produce the lonely crowds and brave new worlds, to modulate the powerful sounds of individuals seeking their own identity.

To Bend Over and Look

Henry David Thoreau once encouraged his listeners to counter a jaundiced view of the world by bending over to see what was behind them—by looking through their legs, hence see the world upside down. One merely has to try this from a public platform to produce explosive laughter, as well as a few boos. I've had enough experience using Thoreau's suggestion in every manner of group—large, intimate, private-public, of different genders and generations—to know that it works! The problem is that most of us flow with the momentum of our lives and don't stop long enough to try searching for enough different perspectives. Naturally enough, we are creatures of habit. At their best the various "encounter" groups concocted since the sixties, a zillion forms of group support and/or therapy, are beyond the fringes of faddism and encourage individuals to develop new perspectives. At their worst, they can be cults demanding conformity. So the question remains: Who is willing to live at the edge of risking discoveries or finding new habits, perspectives, or myths to replace the ones they have; new beliefs into which their old ones can blend or collapse; new ways of seeing, feeling, thinking, touching, tasting, smelling, and intuiting?

Basic Assumptions

In section 2, I discuss what I call "Basic Assumptions Therapy," for it is my belief that most persons must frequently examine the bedrock of their being in order to stay alive, alert, and open to our incredible human potential. Here are some of the assumptions motivating this book:

- We have only begun to penetrate the frontiers of human potential, both mentally and physically (for instance, we're just learning that people in their nineties can recover much of their muscle tone); we don't begin to know the extent to which individuals respond to suggestions (see Shakespeare's *Othello* to illustrate).

- While humans may not be "infinitely perfectible" (an eighteenth-century viewpoint), we may be infinitely malleable and/or mutable.

- Humans have more to gain than lose at any level of development by forming human networks (e.g., the Internet), by sharing insights, by evolving new trust systems, and by accelerating synergistic processes into unique configurations.

- Freedom of inquiry and expression are fundamental values for all persons when expressed without fear of repression, vindictiveness, intimidation, or other forces.

- As Marilyn Ferguson observes in discussing the power of a new paradigm, "You can't defect from an insight; you can't unsee what you have seen."[2] And this might obtain for any other of the human senses, and/or intuition.

- Technologies, such as electronic applications (television, computers, etc.), can be put to positive uses in expanding freedom, self-insight, and self-concept regardless of what has been done thus far; nor do we know the outer limits of those potentials.

- Individuals *can* be in charge of their own lives even under the most dire of circumstances, as witnessed by Victor Frankl's evolution of logotherapy while in a concentration camp during World War II.[3]

- Individuals *can* make a social difference—the John Stuart Mill insight that "if all mankind were of one opinion" that others should not suppress them and vice versa.[4]

- *No* "conventional wisdom" in *any* context is inviolable to critical inquiry or question.

In short, while one must acknowledge the existence of "sacred cows," one need not necessarily milk them! (This would also apply to the above assumptions!)

On Conventional Wisdoms

There is something about a "body of beliefs" or a "body of facts" that makes it sacrosanct in some minds. Yet, as Robert Frost observes in "Mending Wall," "something there is that doesn't love a wall, that sends the frozen-ground swell under it. . . ." And over the years I have found it fascinating to note that Nobel Prizes tend to be awarded to those who drive the ground swell under some of the seemingly solid foundations of science. In fact, the awarding of prizes on the basis of "original contributions" almost requires doubt about or the modification of "conventional wisdoms." Whereas the history of Western philosophy may easily be perceived as "massive verbal retaliation,"[5] the history of modern physics suggests massive "paradigmatic shifts" as a consequence of new viewpoints regarding subatomic particles and the integration of those perspectives into quantum theory. In fact, as Karl Pribram suggests, the very ground we stand on may literally be a figment of our imagination. "Virtual reality" tends to reinforce construction of that figment![6]

It is not very difficult to list, ad infinitum, conventional wisdoms that have been replaced by different (maybe no better or worse, but, indeed, *different*) wisdoms (or even stupidities!). This is no place for an exhaustive list, but citing a few may delineate the parameters of my contention:

- In the field of economics: Adam Smith's (1776) viewpoint regarding nonproductive work simply does not obtain where human services are also a part of the Gross Domestic Product. And we find Smith succeeded by utilitarians who are succeeded by the Marshalites who are succeeded by Keynesians who are in turn succeeded by Milton Friedman's trickle-down economics, who are succeeded by . . . whom?

- In the field of sociology: the inviolability of the nuclear family is "up for grabs" when "family" comes to mean a variety of configurations as well as a whole new language that includes "housemate," "network," and even "tribe." This does not mean that politicians or the public majority necessarily approve of such new definitions, but many folk are challenging old perspectives by putting their bodies where their mouths are.

- In the field of anthropology: we find a "crisis of identity" as once-isolated cultures, too long treated like animals in a zoo, rise up to drive the researchers (voyeurs?) home to investigate their own cultures.

Equally important: examine any field to discover that progress/process must be measured by its resistance or acceptance of such an analysis. While the fission process has separated fields of intellectual endeavor and practical applications—the so-called bifurcation of knowledge—today there is much more inclination to tackle issues from *inter*disciplinary or even *trans*disciplinary viewpoints. Here is a good exercise for any high school or college student, teacher, parent, or business executive: make a list of viewpoints which are now considered valid ("conventional wisdoms"), then file that list away for a year or five to see what happens to those validities . . . and by what criteria.

Let Us Praise Illusion

Since most of us spend the greater portion of our lives doing what *somebody else* wants us to do (parents, teachers, spouses, clergymen, politicians, social mores, etc.), we have all too frequently yielded to commands such as, "Don't daydream, Johnny (Jane)!" or "Pay attention!" or "You gotta face the facts" or "Let's get down to the nitty-gritty" or "Watch the bottom line!" While artists, poets, composers, inventors, social radicals, hermits, and visionaries (among others) have historically resisted such imperatives, only recently have the processes of fantasizing, imaging, or critical thinking come into their own as health-producing activities. Yet, we are still a nation of artistic underachievers and underappreciators, despite museum attendance records, CD sales, and other such statistical indices. One of the first budget cuts of the Reagan administration was that for the National Endowment for the Humanities. Each succeeding administration and Congress has attempted to decimate that budget item even further. Such effort has been consistent with America's pragmatic history. As one post–World War II critic viewed it, "Millions for stadiums but not one cent for Socrates!"

> Aside: Compare this view with that of FDR who sent a whole generation of artists into the cities and towns of America . . . to paint images of everyday incidents and local myths on the walls of public buildings. For instance, while postal patrons in Maine were waiting in lines to buy stamps, they could peruse such murals and identify with persons in lumbering or Main Street scenes. In short, where there was life there was hope and vice versa. While many of these pictures have disappeared under the bulldozers of "progress," one by Waldo Pierce, a friend of Hemingway's, was moved from the Westbrook Post Office to the Portland (Maine) Museum of Art.

As one studies the most recent perceptions of the universe, related to the findings of natural scientists and technologists, and then compares them with the work of artists over the centuries, one discovers a confluence. Generation after generation of artists, extending back to the ancient Egyptians, Greeks, and Chinese, have virtually screamed, "This is the way the world looks." It has included a variety of perceptions of spatial and temporal relationships, light intensities, and psychic interactions between the artist and his subjects. In many ways artists anticipated such phenomena as stroboscopic or intermittent light, and many more so-called contemporary insights. We find that "virtual reality" was anticipated by both ancients and contemporaries.

In short, we should praise illusion as a foundation stone, encourage the childlike temptation to paint/crayon/imagine a world where trees, houses, and humans defy the laws of gravity. It is, indeed, most upsetting to encounter a traditional elementary-school art teacher, as I once did in a graduate education class; she insisted upon and repeatedly proclaimed, loudly and angrily, "My children are going to paint the sky up and the ground down, sky up, ground down."

We have been prone to accept refraction, "meter" recordings of subatomic motions, and synthetic compounds as "real." After all, they "work" empirically and (mostly) in the marketplace. Frequently, too, we'll pay attention to the ventriloquist or magician, the cartoonist or pantomimist because their demonstrations are seemingly bizarre and/or exaggerated to the point of being funny, ridiculous, absurd. Yet who's to say that these phenomena (however critiqued or ridiculed) are at a greater distance from "reality" (for some folk) than that which a majority accepts? And to what extent or under what conditions do we as individuals, as teachers, as parents, as students, as politicians, as interns, or as whosoever . . . as I say, to what degree shall we promote our own illusions in these so-called directions? (See chapter 8.)

As I shall say repeatedly in this book, let us now praise illusion, both famous and ordinary. If we cannot in good conscience do so, let's state clearly why we can't.

To Blossom or Not to Blossom

During the past two or three decades there have been many efforts to "prove" or extol the consequences of opening the human psyche. As James DeWar, Oliver Wendell Holmes, and others have claimed, "Minds are like parachutes, useless unless open." While I cannot stretch quite that far, it is my contention that human blossoming is pretty nigh impossible if one is not open to new and even unpopular ideas, new experiences, new risks, new dilemmas, even new catastrophes. One need only consult any bibliography on learning or humanistic psychology or surf the Internet, to name but three areas of human endeavor, to find provocative books or cyberspaces about the topic. I simply cite the need for not only remaining open to external impulses and inner consequences, but also the imperative for sharing one's reactions to them, somehow, some way, somewhat, somewhen. There is ample evidence that a person internalizes such impulses and consequences via the process of sharing and also that one can make a difference in the lives of others via that sharing. (Note for instance the result of nearly a thousand years of bouncing ideas between tutors and dons at Oxford University!)

Of course there is risk involved. *Of course* a person may be rejected or ridiculed. But as I shall suggest in my discussion of Darwinian theory and creativity (see chapter 6), it is my profoundest conviction that we need as many seeds as we can derive from fertile minds and the plants of experience to effect the mutations for survival and joy.

In specific terms, this is not easy to achieve. But here are some "for instances":

- Whenever an oil tanker sinks or crashes on the shore, whether off the Alaskan coast or Cape Cod, it seems patently obvious that we need a new kind of ship navigator who is not only versed in seamanship but is also environmentally sensitive, one who will not sacrifice the fruits of the sea for the bottom-lining dollar. There seems to be little enthusiasm for that suggestion, probably because current maritime interests are too entrenched to try it.

• Many of us involved in experimental and experiential learning modes have found deaf ears for our insistence that learning is a *process* as well as one delivering *products*. In fact, sometimes *the process IS the product*. Traditionalists continue to use so-called objective, product-oriented, empirical results for their yardsticks. That is, of course, the safest, most practical way. But most disappointing is the fact that evaluators (especially program and institutional accreditors) have been reluctant to acknowledge the existence and function of qualitative modes of analysis and synthesis. Agencies involved in evaluating "life experience" seem more mechanical than organic in their approaches to the problems. Result: accrediting processes have been superficial at best, absurd at worst. (See chapter 3.)

Now, one can, of course, "forget it" and join with the supporters of conventional wisdoms and hope for the best. Or one can listen to her "different drummer" and persist with visions of an open or more inclusive "universe." Yet, every person with a unique angle of vision and belief in human growth must decide whether or not the pains and the prices are worth it. If one listens to William Faulkner's Nobel speech, there is hope that humans will "prevail." Self-development *can* "happen" in the context of a variety of theories and practices.

Yet the question remains, Who is willing to assume the risks? Where does one stand in the vast hinterlands between the rhetorics and realities about uniqueness as a precious phenomenon? And what happens if mavericks, curmudgeons, and dissenters yield to the "politically correct," the "true believers," and the bureaucrats? Whether they yield via inaction or indifference? Or is it possible to minimize brutal *1984* psychology or the subtle *Animal Farm* fascism that George Orwell saw so clearly?

Projections and Prospects

I'd be both blind and dishonest *not* to realize how much projection there is in the beliefs and experiences that I share in this book. I well know the struggle of the dissenter, having lived my beliefs in serving as a catalyst for a dozen or so college generations, serving as a "frontiersman" in innovating graduate programs to "humanize" learning processes. I've also worked with a half-dozen social institutions, training Peace Corps volunteers and encouraging volunteers in creative writing programs; served on condo administrations; done painstaking library archival work; and been responsible for evolving and maintaining the Appalachian and Buckeye Trails as well as trails in my hometown, Saco, Maine. I well know the rejection, alienation, and disappointment in watching institutions sink into power struggles and destruction of the vital impulses that gave them birth—something like watching one's own child battered before one's very eyes.

When John F. Kennedy cited Hemingway's definition of "courage" as "grace under pressure," he knew his references well. That's the kind of courage it takes to follow the vision of individual uniqueness in a social setting or technological application (as with television and computers, for instance) that gobbles up humans. And sometimes they *will* be gobbled by machines and power plays of which they are totally unaware! The history and mystery of the Y2K problems of January 1, 2000, dramatized that "gobbling"!

I shall claim neither too little nor too much, but without fear of much refutation I can point to some harvesting of fruit from my own plantings. As Henry Adams once remarked, "A teacher affects eternity."[7] Hence, anybody engaged in the teaching process—parent, instructor, friend, corporate trainer, ad infinitum—will never *know* their total affect or legacy. There may not even be the proverbial biblical "sign" for which to look. Hence, I'll never *know* my total legacy in conceiving and perpetrating many of my "oddball" ideas. From a humanistic viewpoint, paradoxically enough, I'll stand "on the side of the angels." But to many traditionalists there are probably few bigger fools or devils around. Even a nonparanoid hears the occasional snicker. But I contend that those in my small and relatively intimate arena (more like Fenway Park than Yankee Stadium) know of my existence because I have "made a qualitative difference" in a considerable number of lives. They know, too, of my persistence; my belief in unique angles of vision; my unwillingness to forfeit academic and intellectual freedom, uniqueness of expression, ethical integrity, minority rights, human and humane communication, and other values "civilizations" have spent 2,000 years achieving. I've refused to forfeit them in the name of expediency, power, money, status, and other corroding values. But as I say, I claim neither too much nor too little; there is, after all, a golden mean.

I wrote some sections of this book long before deciding to put it together. Some have been published before (see endnotes). Most ideas have been shared, both orally and in writing, with colleagues, friends, and students as well as a vast landscape of networkers during the past half century. Other sections have evolved recently; therefore, this is a medley of ideas and do-it-yourself suggestions. It may be "a source book of plenitude," as Nathaniel Hawthorne described *Moby-Dick*. My experience tells me that there are many workable ideas and processes upon which anybody may draw, test, or "go forth and do likewise." And surely there's no harm in emulating that which might work or use a notion as a springboard toward further experimentation and/or risking. Although the entire book addresses itself to the fundamental theme of self-awareness and uniqueness, many sections can be read without any practical motivation to borrow or apply. I hope that some of the sections may be "just plain fun."

Postscript

Over the years I have been very fortunate to have exchanged thousands of letters and phone calls with both former and present learners, associates, family, and friends. It would not be difficult to compose a collage of reactions to my being "in the world." As many have observed, with both fiery and gracious candor, "It's next to impossible to be neutral about you. People tend to love or hate you, with nothing in between." And that's probably the major consequence of saying or writing what I think as well as what I feel. I have always prized honest reactions, no matter how much they may have hurt. Students have told me frankly that they would not sign up for my classes or join any enterprise in which I was involved. Why? Because I "challenged their assumptions." Others could not tolerate my predictable unpredictability when asking questions even when I admitted that "dumb questions" were frequently "the best." But one of the reactions I prize most came via a phone call late one night when a friend said, "I've just finished reading your *Person-Centered*

Graduate Education and I find it not only a discussion of alternative ways of learning and knowing but also a philosophy of life." (See chapter 3.) I'm also pleased to have stumbled on "re-FIRE-ment" as a substitute for "re-TIRE-ment"; after all, I was tired enough upon wrapping up a typical work life. To be fired up for the adventure is, indeed, a joyful objective.

It is my fondest hope that those who sample this book will have a similar reaction. Also, I hope they may find a few gems to add to their own treasure-filled journey and its unique qualities. We may all be thankful that there are ample interstices in the grids of power to recognize Lester C. Thurow's insight in "Building Wealth" where he claims, "Great creativity requires hard facts, wild imagination, and nonlogical jumps forward that are then proved to be right by working backward to known principles. Only the rebellious can do it."[8]

Having discussed some of the climates in which persons may exercise their birthright to create as they will (or must!), let us move on to consider some of the basic tools as well as special tools anybody may develop to discover their creative veins.

Notes

1. For a highly readable discussion of the new physics, see Fritjof Capra, *The Turning Point* (New York: Simon & Schuster, 1982).

2. Marilyn Ferguson, *The Aquarian Conspiracy* (Los Angeles: J. P. Tarcher, 1980), pp. 223–24.

3. Viktor Frankl, *Man's Search for Meaning: An Introduction to Logotherapy* (Touchstone, 1984).

4. See John Stuart Mill's "Essay on Liberty."

5. A term coined by Troy Organ, professor of philosophy,

Ohio University. I heard him spin out this notion in a faculty lecture and in personal conversations with him, 1957–1964.

6. Capra, *The Turning Point*, p. 301.

7. Henry Adams, *The Education of Henry Adams* (New York: Modern Library, 1931), p. 300.

8. *Atlantic Monthly* 283, no. 6 (1999): 64ff.

CHAPTER 2

Some Basic Tools

I t's almost a truism to observe that little work can be done without tools. In the everyday, commonsense respect, a carpenter can't build a house without a hammer, saw, and steel square; nor a mason build a fireplace without a trowel and level; nor a mechanic repair a car, boat, or plane without wrenches. Likewise, today's accountants and bankers would be lost without computers; physicists and chemists without atom smashers or centrifuges; medical doctors without pills and powerful imaging machines. Such a list might be endless. But in a more complex sense, this chapter intends to develop a simple manner of differentiating "fact," "opinion," "assumption," and "conclusion" as tools for basic description and analysis.

What Is a Fact?

After years of urging students to think about alternative explanations of whatever a topic might be, I have concluded that

A fact is a function (in the mathematical sense) of the method used to derive it.

For instance a contemporary scientist would use the standard tools of hypothesis, experiment, and observation to derive factual data such as the nature of earth in the backyard or the composition of our moon. This method is usually referred to as "empirical."

A political scientist trying to determine the basic nature of formal or informal power in the United States would muster bushels of data on the who and what of budget making, press the appropriate buttons on her computer to reach her conclusions that such and such was *so* and was based upon facts. Essentially the same method as examining earth in the backyard.

Meanwhile, an advocate of Marxism would begin by setting up a scheme of dialectics wherein a thesis would be opposed by an antithesis; and, after sufficient manipulation of data (facts), the Marxist would conclude with a synthesis. For instance, a worker making X dollars per hour might be opposed by a manager offering X + Y cents per hour. After discussion, negotiation, arbitration, or whatever form of controversy they would choose to use, they might come to what we call a "compromise." But—an important "but"—this framework would continue indefinitely as the way to resolve an economic and a political struggle, all within the context of class warfare. In short, any data or facts used must be perceived within the conclusion about the inevitable arrival of that classless society. Any data or fact must fit into or be derived through that logical/dialectical system. Critics, especially empiricists, might insist that the Marxist starts with his conclusion.

In a similar vein, look at the essential methods of the evolutionist and the creationist. Whereas a fact for the latter might be a quote from the Bible (e.g., God created heaven and earth in seven days), the followers of Charles Darwin would muster facts or characteristics regarding species to support the position that the earth evolved via various processes over millions of years.

Without flogging the proverbial dead horse, one may choose

any body or organized collection of so-called facts (animals grow different-sized necks; the Founding Fathers had many problems designing the U.S. Constitution, as illustrated in the *Federalist Papers*), then subject the collection of data to analysis to determine how they were derived.

The daily newspaper and television news are also superb laboratories for anybody wishing to test their skills in differentiating facts from opinions as well as seeing for themselves the implications of their analysis. I've always enjoyed needling both learners and associates about using the sports section of any newspaper as a source of both hard data and opinions. When a paper reports that the Superbowl score was 35 to 21 or the seventh World Series game result was 4–2, one *knows* that those are irrefutable facts . . . ones that can be checked empirically to ascertain their *truth*! But if a sportswriter claims that Vince Lombardi and Don Shula were the best coaches ever guiding professional football teams (an opinion), one wonders what facts led the writer to that conclusion? Why? Because as Bertrand Russell observed in his "New Decalogue," "Have no respect for the authority of others, for there are always contrary authorities to be found."[1] The question is, Upon what basis does an "authority" claim to be an authority? And what are the facts of the matter?

Again, one could choose any topic in any newspaper to check a writer's facts versus her opinions via the process of such an analysis, whether applied to facts or authority. Although journalists of every media boast about "having the facts," the most superficial analysis will reveal their results as being tainted by their opinion or a viewpoint unsupported by facts. It's as though those with differing opinions or conclusions were saying, "Don't confuse me with the facts because I've made up my own kind." I once lectured to and discussed this topic at a school of journalism where the students didn't have the slightest idea about the process of thought they were using to derive what they called "facts." One only needed to press them a little and their papier-mâché conclusions collapsed like the proverbial house of cards.

A fact in the commonsense use of the term is a statement that can be verified by observation or readily obtained documentation. I can safely say that my friend Nancy married my friend Bill on June 14, 1992. I can also use an apparatus of proof, reliable documentation, etc., to substantiate my report of the fact that they were indeed married on that day. Critics might ask, "Isn't it your opinion that they are your friends?" and, of course, I'd have to work on that!

An opinion, on the other hand, is an expressed belief. If, for instance, it were noised around that Nancy and Bill eloped because she were pregnant and I chose to believe that as well as express a view that it were true, my opinion would need checking, however difficult that might be.

(Those seeking further clarification of these points need only consult in-depth discussions of scientific methodology.)

Speaking of "truth": I am ever skeptical of those claiming to be searching for "*the* truth" even if they do not capitalize or stress the word. Most often they assume that the reader or listener knows the grounds on which the search and/or the conclusions are reached. During the O. J. Simpson murder case and the presidential impeachment, both members of Congress and lawyers for *all* sides mentioned the search for "the truth" thousands of times, failing to explain that a "truth" established by legal means is a particular kind of truth ramified and justified by rigid "rules of evidence" which are not always so self-evident. TV commentators and anchor folk also commit this omission with regularity, an omission that certainly does not make their listeners any more sophisticated as informed and/or concerned citizens. My effort to get the participants on CNN's *Burden of Proof* program (1999) to help educate their listeners in this regard seemed to result only in . . . *silence.* Hence, it's important to be aware of one's own basis of fact. Anybody can express an opinion whenever he wishes if he doesn't mind facing objections. Many controversies start that way.

Basic Assumptions Therapy

Thus far I have encouraged the perception of facts in the context of the methods used to derive them. Those who are intellectually curious or simply curious by nature will immediately see the connections between facts and assumptions or taking a viewpoint for granted.

Mr. Andrew Macfarlane, discussing the resurgence of creationist "scientists," warns in a letter to *Harper's* magazine against perpetuating

> the dangerous misconception that science is the enemy of religion.
>
> Once, the abandonment of reason and the embrace of superstition led us into the Dark Ages. It is vital that we not let [such] "scientists" . . . lead us down that road again.[2]

One might easily discuss the conflicts between the assumptions of mainstream Western science and the assumptions of the Western Church. Again, there are whole sections of libraries filled with the controversial discussion and evidence of the assumptions of each. If one does, indeed, stick to the Genesis account of God's creating the world in the proverbial "week," then that assumption of "fact" alone necessitates a different analysis of fossil records and the "origins of species." To understand the time lag of the move from an earth-centered (geocentric) view of our universe to a sun-centered (heliocentric) view, one need only look at Galileo's experience. The Church required more than three centuries to accept his perceptions as found through a telescope . . . a basic tool in his discovery of facts! To this day it is enlightening to inquire, "Why are there relatively few Catholic scientists?" What kind of basic assumptions therapy would be required to change the Church's appeal to the authority of its own tradition to an appeal to empirical facts?

We frequently hear the comment "Don't confuse me with the facts, I've made up my own mind." As noted above, my own variation on that theme is to substitute for "mind" the word "kind." To me, this suggests the value in weighing the basic assumptions upon which one's "mind" is made up as well as the "facts" derived therefrom. Obvious as it may be, perhaps it's time to note that the mind is a tool. And unfortunately, the "true believer"[3] in her approach to either facts or assumptions tends to *limit* her viewpoint to one set of assumptions with a "body of facts" that permit neither the perception nor conception of alternative viewpoints, nor knowledge of the methods to derive alternative viewpoints. Hence, it is possible that basic assumptions therapy or weighing alternatives is truly impossible in such situations. And, of course, this virtually rules out any other MIND-ing of any topic or perception. We know humans use the mind only to an infinitesimal percentage of its potential. But once a human becomes a "true believer," no matter the topic or on right or left ends of a continuum, then that percentage is narrowed even more; and, if this is restricted to some type of cult, either secular or spiritual, then that narrowing is long term.

Hence, those truly concerned about widening their realm of creativity do well to make a list of basic assumptions regarding: marriage, life and death, religion, government, and education.

You name the topic . . . then ask how such assumptions can be changed in the direction of expanding their own human potential. It may require courage to seek new viewpoints from somebody who is known to take diametrically opposing viewpoints . . . or consult a facilitator of change . . . or a group whose viewpoint and dialogue are radically different than your own. With so many support groups available to the average person, this should not be too difficult to achieve, but indeed, it will take guts!

But the basic goal is to free oneself, as the eighteenth-century German philosopher Immanuel Kant once did when he spoke of the English philosopher David Hume's freeing him from his "dogmatic slumbers." It is doubtful if any person is so free of habit and assumptions that she can avoid searching for such freedom, painful as it may be.

Exercise No. 1: Facts versus Assumptions

Perhaps it's time to check the utility of my viewpoint. Richard Dawson, writing for the *Chronicle of Higher Education*, observed that, "We are survival machines, robot vehicles blindly programmed to preserve the selfish molecules known as genes."[4]

Whether you agree with Dawson or not, you are certainly free to test my views about facts, opinions, and assumptions against your own perceptions; so take your own tools, along with a red pen, to your local newspaper and television. Do you find "responsible" use of facts? Irresponsible? Something in between?

What about assumptions and conclusions? Compare essays on the op-ed pages or TV editorials with those by the journalists.

It is said that we live in the era of the sound bite (tiny pieces of information which can be chewed quickly). Can you identify what is meant by that opinion/assumption/ fact? If not, compare the information and the style of the newspaper *USA Today*, with those of the network commentators (Brokaw, Rather, Jennings), also your favorite "big-time" papers such as the *New York* or *Los Angles Times, Washington Post, Chicago Tribune, Boston Globe, Miami Herald,* etc.

Aside: You will find it valuable to read Margo Morgan's *Mutant Message Down Under.* An MD, she went to Australia to bring Western medicine with its particular brands of assumptions, applications, and "truths" to the Aborigines. Before she returned to the United States, her immersion in a completely different culture convinced her of the folly of her assumptions. I had a similar experience in Greece: using my New England values and grids, I was ready to write a book after being there for three weeks; by the time I returned home, I knew I couldn't do it in three years. Simply living and encountering students there for a year served as my basic assumptions therapy. I gained new perspectives and never returned to my "dogmatic slumbers" or the unexamined opinions on which I was reared.

Do-It-Yourself Kits 1

Over the years I have written a large number of "do-it-yourself" kits, such as Countdown to Re-FIRE-ment, Haiku Writing, Reviving Controversy, and so on. Many have been spoofs. Others have been serious efforts to suggest a different angle of vision for solving a human problem, or seeking a different perspective on a human endeavor. One kit has grown from a very practical means of capturing pieces/chunks/gems/atoms of human experience some of which are often difficult to "catch." It's my Writing-in-the-Dark Kit. Actually, it grew out of the frustration I felt in capturing/recording my dreams, and I stumbled onto the method early one morning when renting a strange house in Putney, Vermont. I had a powerful dream which, upon nearly "waking," seemed to convey an important message. I kept my eyes closed and stumbled to a nearby bureau where I knew there was paper and pen. With eyes still closed, I began to block print an account of the dream. The pad of paper on which I was writing was four inches by six inches, the size I usually use to record research notes. Hence, I had to turn the pages as my recording of the dream went on and on. I returned to bed without opening my eyes, then lay there reflecting upon the dream, running it as one might rerun a video or movie to review its salient features or most prominent images. Right there was born the technique that I've built into the Writing-in-the-Dark Kit as follows:

1. Take several pieces of standard 8½" × 11" paper, preferably the smoothest/slipperiest that you can find, and cut them into four parts from which you can make a stack or pad (scrap paper is OK). Do *not* staple the papers together.
2. Place this "pad" on a table by your bedside so that you can reach it with a minimum amount of disturbance of your

sleep. It is assumed that you will most often use this process at night or when in bed.

3. Bring the "pad" over onto your chest where you may write comfortably, again disturbing your sleep the least . . . all this without opening your eyes. (It will be easiest for right-handed persons to do this; left-handers may wish to experiment with a "best" position.)

4. Grasp the top left-hand side of the pad with your left hand, so that your thumb will lap over the edge of the paper a quarter to half an inch and hence be a reference position as you begin to write, bringing the pen or pencil against your thumb.

5. Then begin to record your dream, your description of the imaging you are doing, your fantasies, your poems, your outline of an itinerary which you want to record; capture your bright idea, a new musical composition, an invention, or whatever. And record via BLOCK PRINTING rather than cursive where it's difficult to cross *t*'s, dot *i*'s, make loops, etc., in the dark! Even if you do not connect every line of every letter, you'll still be able to read your recording when you choose to wake up.

6. Spacing: as you write and approach the right edge of the page and wish to move back to the left side, move your thumb down a half inch or so in order to position your pen against it and begin the second line. Repeat for lines 3, 4, etc., to the bottom of the page. If you need more than one page, simply bring the completed page(s) against your chest and try to remember to write the number of the new page at the top of the next page and next, each time tucking the completed pages against your chest.

7 At first you may feel a bit constrained by the size of your paper, but once used to the process you'll get used to the "feel" of the space available.

8. Once completing the recording of whatever you want to save, grasp the completed page and slip it from the pad (hence the importance of slippery paper and the importance of not stapling it or using a commercially glued writing pad), then toss the completed page(s) to the floor beside your bed . . . with minimum awareness; you may wish to record another dream, write another poem or whatever.

9. When you've become accustomed to this "in-the-dark activity," you'll probably be aware enough to record the current date at the bottom of the page; until then, when you get out of bed, record the current date. You might want to use the material in a journal or file in chronological order or find some other important reason for having the date. I've also developed my own code for the time of day; e.g., A (before getting out of bed); S (at siesta time); P (evening); M (upon retiring). In fact, such a code enabled me to make several self-studies about creative awareness.

10. Although locating do-it-yourself activity at bedside, I have also found writing in the dark helpful for making notes or writing haiku and free verse at the movies or while watching videos; in the margins of my notepad while seeming to pay attention to proceedings of a meeting (cf. section on "Grooks" in chapter 6). It is a surefire method to capture some levels of your consciousness without disturbing others.

Simple as it may sound, I've "taught" this method to groups in hands-on contexts at seminars and colloquiums, and also to many persons on a one-to-one basis. All one needs is a dark room and the willingness to learn. No doubt, it's a surefire approach to tapping inner depths of creative ideas, events, etc. Ironically enough, I've had former students/learners bubble, "Writing in the dark is the most important thing you ever taught me!" Flattered, grateful, or dismayed as I might be upon hearing such a remark, I sometimes smile and observe, "More than you learned from all those 'brilliant lectures' (!) and discussions growing out of years and years of reading and thinking?" After embarrassing snickers, the usual response: a considered "Yes!"

"Perchance to Dream"

Obviously, like any other tool, the skill of writing in the dark must be kept well honed. While not imperative to write in the dark every night, it does help to practice using the process until it "comes naturally." Regardless of the dream theory you may hold, we know enough about recording dreams, too, to observe that writing them down, even in fragments, is somewhat like priming the pump. Even people who claim they've not dreamed before now indicate this process has been enabling. Likewise, persons who say they can't write poetry may wish to try another suggestion; namely, close the eyes and cast some images on their mental screen, then record what is seen. Do it in color and in whatever sequence the moment demands, then write about it. No question, it liberates if it gets images to flow. Ironically enough, as King Lear discovered after he'd blinded himself, one frequently "sees" better in the dark than in the light. This is *not* to suggest dangerous experiments in sense-deprivation, but the typically curious person may find en-LIGHT-en-ment via deliberately pretending to be blind, deaf, dumb, and numb—not competing with persons with those "limitations," but rather using this process to gain appreciation and empathy for the values and the burdens of such modifications to consciousness. It has been my discovery, too, that my own consciousness as well as that of many of my associates has been expanded by such experimentation.

Crap Detecting as a Way of Life

A journalist once asked Ernest Hemingway what was required to be a "great writer." The famous novelist responded that he "must have a built-in, shockproof crap detector."[5]

I constructed a do-it-yourself kit around the concept of "crap detecting," with a variety of recommendations, including:

1. Find a secluded place, in a woods or a corner of a jet plane, and scream a thousand times, "Never say never" or your own name or a particularly distasteful four-letter word. In a short time you'll discover the absurdity of finding some words obnoxious. This is a conditioner for four-dimensional, linguistic appreciation of words that sometimes repel, especially the four-letter ones.
2. Practice crap detecting. Read a newspaper with a red pen in hand. One day mark adjectives, on another adverbs, etc. In December 1968, for instance, after watching President Nixon introduce his cabinet and being struck by his seeming egocentricity, I picked up the *New York Times* and circled more than one hundred *I*'s, *my*'s, and *mine*'s from his printed speech, confirming my belief that one can bulldoze walls from ears.
3. Sharpen your listening and analytical powers by listening to social commentary on audio- or videotape where you can rerun questionable statements; learn to distinguish between fact and opinion; hear fallacies, cause-and-effect

      misconceptions, or short-circuiting. Find evidence of insufficient evidence. Learn to distinguish irony and paradox. (For more on these topics see chapter 4.)

4. Keep a log or journal in which you record both seeing and hearing experiences, and differentiate fact and opinion. Dialogue with talk-show hosts and participants. In short, direct your crap-detecting equipment toward your environment so that you can check your own process and progress from the work of your own brain and hand. (See chapter 2 for more on journaling.)

5. Fill your home with mottoes, posters, etc., any environmental support to reinforce your efforts. One motto that you must "pin up" in neon lights, especially if you hold a socially relevant job and/or regard yourself as a critic, heretic, or dissenter; namely, TO BE OF USE YOU MUST TAKE ABUSE. Few societies or subsocieties tolerate, let alone honor, those taking such roles!

6. Construct for yourself other kinds of kits to test your characteristics and views of the world. For instance, doesn't every egomaniac require a Do-It-Yourself Messiah Kit or the misanthrope need a Do-It-Yourself Scapegoat Kit? If you can construct such kits to include your own foibles and come out laughing, you'll have little difficulty with crap detecting. No matter the topic, you can sharpen your sensitivity and perception of your relationships to friends and community.

7. Structure your own film festival, watch a number of videos in one evening, then with watch in hand, determine how long it takes you to miss the commercials during the next film you see, off network TV.

A former black colleague once recounted how often he'd been called "paranoid" because of his ability to set himself in almost any context and use his crap detector with keen analysis. His conclusion, "Hell, I'm not paranoid, I'm just damned sensitive to my environment." One doesn't have to read much Hemingway to appreciate his requirement for defining the great writer or finding ways to test one's own capacity to perceive the world around her.

Some Things I Do to Get Things Done

The distance between planning to *do* something and actually *doing it* is sometimes vast. Measuring that distance helps put action into perspective. I'm not too sure that I thought very much about it until one of my doctoral students asked, "What do you do to get things done?" Such a simple question, I thought. But I agonized when building a bridge over the chasm the question suggested. It required reflection. It required putting aside assumptions about whether or not I had actually done anything of any creative worth. I also wrestled with my ego! It required several drafts before I could share the writing with my learners and colleagues in 1973. And even as I face a new revision, I may further reconstruct the basic guidelines. As with my initial response to the learner,

I TRY . . .

- *not* to remember details that aren't worth remembering; rather, for economy's sake, I scribble them on four-by-six-inch pads of paper and leave them in some place where I'll "fall over them" and *do* what I instruct myself to do. With no secretarial assistance it helps to keep works in process and/or *to be done* out in open spaces where I can see them. If things get filed, they're out of sight, out of mind!

- to keep the open spaces pretty large in physical terms; in my study or in any temporary workspace, the floor is literally littered with scraps of paper, piles which constitute particular projects to be done, things to be read, videos to be seen, and so on. Sometimes there are slips of paper strewn along the floor in lines ten or fifteen feet long (letters to be mailed, phone calls to be made). My object is to keep things to be done *in sight* and (in general) within my own private spaces (except for a foot or two into the hall) in such a way that I keep a "graphic view" of these needs as well as their relative importance. Then, too, seemingly inefficient, other trigger scraps of paper, kept in fairly small numbers of piles remind me of particular projects, possible action. I don't necessarily keep such files narrowly categorized but sufficiently "under control" to make it relatively easy to find specific items. I joke about my "piling system"!

- to keep my sense of "time geography," past, present, and future, rather keenly honed; hence, phone logs of long-distance phone calls, calendars nearby or in my breast pocket, timing of "things to be done" set as tentative dates "in my head"; fortunately, I remember dates fairly easily, both events to be held and events which occurred one, two, five, ten, twenty, thirty years ago in some kind of graphic sense . . . to keep a time perspective. While in advancing years I don't have as much "control" of such time perspectives as I once did, but, using associative techniques and a few "crib notes," I can usually come close.

- to use a kind of blocking technique in scheduling certain kinds of events; attempting to block appointments together, classes back-to-back, nuts-and-bolts events side-by-side, shopping chores done sequentially. This leaves large open blocks of time for reading, writing, or other kinds of activity which take larger chunks (it is absurd to start serious writing or reading if one has only fifteen minutes). In other words, part of the skill of getting things done is to allocate appropriate events to appropriate times . . . even allowing ample opportunity for spontaneity to occur.

- to employ my lifelong "habit" of thinking the opposite of whatever a decision or explanation might be. Perhaps it grew from my tendency to contradict, for my parents frequently charged me with being "contradictory" and said that I "always wanted the last word." Perhaps that is the root of the dialectic. But without being mechanistic about it, I find it helpful to consider an entire range of alternatives along a continuum or into the cornices or crevices of a gestalt before "making a decision" or "taking a course of action." Presumably that's what citizens are "supposed to do" before voting or making lifesaving or life-threatening decisions . . . even deciding upon disposition of their bodies at the time of death! There isn't always time or inclination to make such decisions systematically; but, if one develops the "habit" (?) of considering alternatives, on the spot, in the long haul it is a mind-set which is invaluable in doing split-second thinking (the mind preceded the computer), and Hemingway no doubt built this into his "crap detector."

Most importantly:

- Never work for too long a period on one project or topic; no matter the pressure, walk around a bit periodically.

- Take a brief (fifteen to twenty minutes at the most) siesta ("power nap") every afternoon, no matter the pressure!

- When possible *do* most things immediately and you'll only have to do them *once*; occasionally do not do a task to prove to yourself that *not* to *do*, paradoxically, is to *do*!

Then, watching chinks of time:

- Learn to fill them with spontaneous haiku, grooks, searching for paradoxes and ironies (see later chapters on these topics).

- To keep some kind of balance, continue to remind yourself that humor and seriousness need balance since life is sometimes too absurd to be taken seriously.

Exercise No. 2: Motivation and Health

- Make a list of things you do to get things done as well as fail to accomplish.

- Do you find any correlations between "doing things" and your health?

- Do you laugh enough? Why? Why not?

- Make a list of your own creations (large or small). About which do you feel most satisfaction? Why? Can you recreate your state of mind and health when you accomplished this, whether making a dress or kitchen table, perfecting a new golf grip, writing a poem, composing a long-overdue letter . . . again, it matters not how large or small.

- Can you locate the core of your motivation and invent ways to make it more vital; reduce the stumbling blocks; lubricate it with laughter, meditation, moments congenial to your own creative being?

Journaling

During the past decade or two an increasing number of persons have "discovered" journaling (logging/diary keeping/duo-logging) as a vital route to self-development. It has become an important life-giving, learning process, too. While for centuries, folk like the Puritans as well as writers such as Samuel Pepys have kept diaries, the "movement" in recent years is different than earlier ones; not necessarily better or worse, but different. For instance, while Puritan ancestors used the process as "keepers of their conscience," most people today utilize the method as "keepers of consciousness." It is tempting to ascribe causality to the more recent efforts. Possibly there are as many reasons why persons do it as there are persons. No doubt residents in early Massachusetts did it at the prompting of the clergy. Today, in what might be called the Psychological Age, the push toward self-awareness and self-development has the power of a tidal wave, hence any tool that can be used to achieve that end (no matter its quality or quantity) seems appropriate. Group facilitators encourage it. Some doctors endorse it. Teachers use it to stimulate their students to improve power for both inner and outer observation. Corporations likewise. And, of course, inventors, composers, writers, and other artists have for centuries used journals for collecting thoughts, processing ideas, sketching choreographic insights, and developing paintings and architectural notions. A scientist's notebook may have similar functions; for instance Leonardo Da Vinci's notebooks reflect some of the origins of modern science and technology as well as artistic insights. Even a contemporary scientist's lab notes could be regarded as a journal if she reflected continuing activity.

Any person at the dawn of his creative life may wish to explore the journal as a basic tool. Libraries are filled with books on the topic. Practitioners of the method will always have tips about the "best way" to go about it. After spending a "comfortable" amount of time seeing what others have done, past and present, the beginner may learn the most via a hands-on approach. I prefer to purchase a blank book of whatever size, color, or texture that seems best for current activities. I lean toward the blank book rather than a lined one simply so I can write, sketch, attach pictures, theater tickets, typed notes, letters, and so on, without the suggestion of limitations that lines connote. You're not boxed in. In short, your journal can become a potpourri of those items which reflect your own interests and experiences. As one friend exclaimed, "The journal is *you*!"

Another tip: find a quiet place away from the telephone, television, doorbell, family, or other intruding external forces or events to review whatever you've included. During the early phases, *read at one sitting* so that you may be objective about your subjectivity. After all, it is your life; your journal that you are assessing. Only *you* can ascertain whether or not it begins to reflect *your* life or suggests directions of change. You may wish to prepare a list of questions that you expect to answer with such a reading/browsing; such questions as "Does it make sense? Is this *me* . . . or am I keeping this for posterity or with a particular reader in mind? Somebody else's views? Do I wish to share? Am I putting self-imposed limitations on what I'm doing? Does this further my purposes? Restrict them? What insights about my life are worth more thought? More recording and recoding? Am I willing to change, transform my own life?"

If, after you've given yourself an adequate amount of time both to keep and to reflect upon your journal and you wish to find a creative comparison for such an endeavor, you may wish to look at Elyse N. Rapaport's *Creative Choices*: *Finding Meaning as Your Life Changes*.[6] There you will find her discussing at length ways and means to deal with Creation, Conception, Choice, Change, Contrast, Crisis, Commitment, Catalyst, Camelot, and Continuity (she's fond of "*C*'s"!). You may find and prefer other models. Possibly you'll find examples on the Internet which will speak to your need for relevance and immediacy. The point is: Don't give up easily. The purpose of journaling is to triangulate your own path and what's happening on it.

Duo-logging

This is a variation on a theme. Several decades ago one of my more creative Antioch master's students and I dreamed up what we believed was a unique exercise to see what we could learn from it. We agreed to write a certain number of paragraphs *about* logging/journaling and to do it independently of one another, then to combine our paragraphs, interspersing them one after the other. So we went our separate ways to do our "pieces," then met to read them aloud in alternating patterns. Upon finishing, we looked at each other in surprise. Only two of them needed to be shifted around in order to avoid an anachronism. So we set up the dialogue as a duo-logue. In many ways it was a combination of definitions or viewpoints. While most of it appears in my *Person-Centered Graduate Education,* here are a couple of pairs of Joanne's and my interactions[7]:

> J: What is a log? the almost-caught-it-on-paper . . . a file folder of papers, bits and pieces . . . explosions . . . the hate letter that was never sent . . . wondering . . . wanderings . . .

> R: Log writing can include anything you do, from the very intimate to the very public. After all, if you're doing it for self-catharsis; for developing self-motivation; for improving your ability to clarify, for the record; for sharpening your communications skills; what does it matter that it contains only those things which you're against? (. . . a hint of irony and paradox?)

> J: There is something that wants saying . . . somewhere under something . . . it is struggling to be heard . . . and not to be heard . . . it is shy of exposure, fearful of light.

> R: He thought my views
>   were very snide
>   it seemed that I'd hit
>   his holy pride.

Our yes-no motions
put us in boxes
parliamentarians
slyer than foxes . . .

We circulated our Duologue among our Antioch colleagues and colearners, had some very productive discussion on the topic, and moved on. It proved to be a basic tool to trigger thought and action in our seminars.

Letter Writing as a Portal to Self-Development

Many of my former students sometimes despaired of journal keeping as a means of communicating with their muses, finding it difficult to write for or to themselves. A psychologist or philosopher might call that process narcissistic or self-serving. But I have frequently recommended that those interested in the result but skeptical of the process might find a similar result by corresponding with a trusted friend, a person to whom he could say practically anything, perhaps using the model of the "father confessor" or "mother superior." The psychological result might be similar despite the danger of writing what one believes some-body else wants to hear! If one chooses such a method as a basic tool, then it's important to keep copies of each letter so that at some appropriate time (a month, a year, or longer) the writer could make a penetrating analysis of the "file," asking questions comparable to those mentioned above when reflecting upon a journal. There might be one more advantage in the letter-writing approach; namely, ask the trusted person his reaction to the same questions you ask yourself. What changes does he perceive?

Another tip: work out ground rules with that trusted person, rules such as privacy, frequency, and length of letters, lest the task for the reader be overwhelming (as mine did once when a person wrote to me daily and expected a quick response); in fact, the issue of expectation is rather crucial. Develop clearly defined rules about that, lest the interaction go off the track when one person has different expectations than the other.

Although this is the era of the telephone, computer, and fax, I have used both letter writing and journaling as basic tools in my own self-development as well as a source of plenitude. In correspondences spanning two to five decades, I have observed an improved ability to express my viewpoints, a growing openness in saying what I think, a clarity in distinguishing between personal and professional communication, a sharpening of observation powers, a greater command of English vocabulary, and a greater sense of the joy of writing, thinking, and communicating. Also, just as grading the first ten thousand student exams was more difficult for me than the second ten thousand, writing the first twenty-five thousand letters was more difficult than the second twenty-five thousand!

Some sample insights:

- from one twenty-year correspondence, I developed greater self-confidence in my own self-worth and intelligence, motivation to attend college against all financial odds; after she married a Chinese fellow during World War II, more sensitivity and knowledge about the struggle between Nationalist and Communist China; more appreciation of a female viewpoint in the pre–feminist era;

- from a twenty-five-year exchange with a man who team-taught with me: knowledge and appreciation of John Dewey's philosophy, skills in applying and articulating alternative methodologies, subtleties of artistic photography. In addition: the joy of receiving and writing no fewer than a letter or two a month for all those years and developing a warm relationship with a vital human being, involved in some of the important political issues of the day;

- from a fifty-year exchange with a musician who taught me the foundations of classical music, I enhanced my increased understanding and appreciation of jazz as well as organ building, courage in battling emphysema and a wife with incipient Parkinson's; also, continuing contact with two sons evolving their lives in the music world, one enhancing human appreciation of food and music at the international level and the other becoming a treasure in France for his entertaining and drawing children into sounds they might never have imagined;

- from a sixty-year exchange with a high-school classmate, learning about some of the intricacies of Washington bureaucracy, reflections of regret over his early athletic prowess as related to health, but courage (grace under pressure) in offering himself as a guinea pig in Parkinson's research.

And, of course, viewed from the vantage point of decades rather than mere months and years, these changes are more easily ascertained. This is not to say "trust me, I have the truth"; rather, it is to encourage persons to experiment with these tools and gauge the result much as one might treat a saw or an electric drill or a car jack: how well does it work? I would not exchange this correspondence for all the best-sellers and prizes in the world.

Listening with a Third Ear

No doubt you've encountered persons whom you felt needed "listening lessons," the person so enamored with her own voice that that voice served as a shield, barrier, turn-off (use any metaphor which you regard as appropriate). Possibly a friend will tell you whether or not you fit into that category.

Except as we may recall our elementary-school teachers telling us, "Johnny, pay attention!" or "Jane, be quiet!" not too much schooling is devoted specifically to listening . . . though it does happen when sensitive teachers or school nurses discover hearing defects. Yet, insofar as we are conscious of extreme cases or teachers chastising schoolchildren, it is simply assumed that being able to hear is a norm. While that may be generally true when it comes to sound in and of itself, it is probably inadequate if one wishes to become a specialist in the nuances of intonation, accent, and meaning. One is reminded of James Thurber's fable, "The Weaver and the Silk-worm."[8] When the weaver met a silkworm, he asked, "What are you doing with that stuff?"—a remark that the silkworm interpreted as a put-down. Thurber observes that following the dialogue each creature went his own way, thinking that each had insulted the other. No doubt we all misinterpret intended meaning in every imaginable way. I am no audiologist, but I am an amateur student of listening and suggest here a few creative ways to give oneself listening lessons if one does not wish to consult experts in the field:

- Tape your own voice, either alone or in a group context, then ask the simple question: How do I sound? What needs do I have to get myself "over the footlights" to reveal the persona that I intend? And, if in a group context, did my intent get across? If so, why so? If not, why not? You may wish to chart your message. And what do you learn about your listening power when you respond to associates?

- Using a camcorder, try the same "exercise" to assess your ability to be clear as well as hear. If you want your efforts to have practical results, do oral histories to capture biographies and local events. It is my contention that everybody has a story to tell *if there's somebody who will listen!*

- Having analyzed and reflected your own listening skills, ask a trusted friend, one whom you perceive as a "good listener," to use her skills on you and be frank about what she hears.

- Extend your own inquiries to dialogue on television and in films. What constitutes effective dialogue? What destroys it? Try writing dialogue, then speaking it.

The objective of these various exercises is not necessarily to become a professional speaker or listener, but to become one effective in using your voice and listening powers to achieve your professional and personal goals.

The computer, too, can serve as a basic tool of communication. Assuming your computer has the appropriate range of voice and vision, there are limitless opportunities to see, hear, imagine, and articulate to shape and sharpen hearing skills as well as those involving the other senses. The best part of using that tool: one may sit in one's own household and extend ears and eyes to the world, encounter other languages and the "voices" of other cultures. There is little need to experience embarrassment and/or be limited by unfamiliarity with diverse languages and cultures when one may seek (and find) so many outlets. It is only "natural" to be hesitant or shy when encountering new phenomena, but one need not be threatened by it with so many means to polish the burrs from one's own hesitations.

I once met a man, Benjamin F. Thompson, a professor of psychology and education at Antioch College. We began our relationship by working closely together for three months, and I observed his uncanny ability to listen. Using his own assumptions about human development and the learning process, he certainly had more angles of analysis than I'd ever dreamed could exist. He could listen at several levels, i.e., he heard the words others spoke. He heard the plea of "Help" or need for attention from a simple story. He also heard the voice of "impotence" from a spoken autobiography. He measured the *quality* of fear from the *quantity* of words. In short, he had the skills of a competent therapist and perceived learning as a kind of therapy. While I did not rub elbows with him as closely during our next seventeen years of collegiality, I did watch, listen, communicate, share perceptions of common experiences, and evaluate those perceptions. I have frequently remarked that "I served a seventeen-year listening apprenticeship with Ben." Although he is now dead, I can still see the twinkle in his eye resulting from my perceptions and analysis of our joint serving on master's and doctoral committees. In addition to listening, I read many of the books that he recommended and we discussed their content. It changed my listening patterns, not to become a clone but to develop basic tools. At one point I did some self-exploration and experimenting which was potentially dangerous. I speculated: If "schizophrenia" suggests split personality and hence split listening, was it not logical that listening at more than two levels would be "polyphrenia"? But it was one thing to speculate and *know*, but another to experiment. At one point in time I attempted to listen, as Ben did, at four or five levels of consciousness more or less simultaneously. I could do pretty well with three or four, but my understanding fragmented at five. Ben was very sensitive to such dangers and warned me about them, knowing the potential dangers from psychedelic drugs. I listened, but I pushed on, not with drugs but with a grim determination to explore. But when the fragmenting began, I knew it was time to quit. The exploration, however, did enable me to develop some basic guidelines for listening at both surface and less obvious levels. Ben taught me to hear word inflection, watch body language, and understand what these told me about the persons and their needs. In short, much as writing haiku and amateur painting sharpens one's sense of color, form, and other subtleties while encountering nature, so does listening with the proverbial "third" ear enhance human understanding. One needs to do it, somewhat as a clinical matter, and have a reliable guide by one's side.

Question as Tool

It's a rare person whose intellectual or "natural" curiosity doesn't evoke or provoke a question to satisfy that curiosity with some kind of data whether it's about the score of a game, tomorrow's weather, or another person's age. In point of fact: we bathe daily in questions throughout our lives. Yet, there are many cultural inhibitors that block us from asking certain questions. We are conditioned to refrain from entering certain areas of discourse; for instance, in some eras in white middle-class society, it's a norm *not* to discuss religion and politics, but that limits inquiry. Likewise, asking a woman's age. If we push our curiosity too far, we are warned via epithet that "curiosity killed the cat"!

At the other end of the inquiry spectrum, scholars are trained to ask questions. At the extreme end, scientists may question conventional wisdom to obtain data which may eventually change natural laws which could lead to new hypotheses that result in new data that leads . . . ad infinitum. Likewise, scholars in other disciplines follow hunches; search for clues; assemble bodies of information about individuals, social groups, and political activities. And *all* of this activity may result from a single question which leads, leads, and leads some more. The mode of asking questions via polls varies from scientific to fine art.

It is a fact of tragic dimension that children's questions are so often deferred by parents, teachers, ministers, and other adults. When a typical child asks, "Who created God?" or is curious about their own body parts, all too frequently the parent or teacher resorts to the sidetracking process: "You'll know when you grow up!" Also historically, the truly curious child has defied adult "authorities" and learned by himself or from another child, sometimes from dubious sources (about sex from "behind the barn," about smoking or drugs "trying them on the sly"). But we have entered an era where these dams to curiosity will not stop its flow, in fact they may hasten it. When children at any age have access to computers, they merely need to put their questions to the computer by filling in a few words that they want searched, whether it's "God," "cancer," "space," or some other human endeavor.

The forces that foster human ignorance, that seek to defer questions, are diminishing in both quality and quantity. Hence, the power of the question as tool. And as the presence of the computer and its connections to the Internet improves, the power to hide information that will encourage "dogmatic slumbers" will also diminish. It surely is not a simple task to distinguish between the "true" and the distorted, fact and opinion. This may be a major hazard as we stand at the threshold of the super age of inquiry, or in many ways its democratization.

Now, what millions of people will *do* with the answers to their questions is an interesting question all its own. We also live in the age of informational overkill. So much data is being developed so rapidly that no one person can possibly absorb it all, nor can any one group, as for instance, the faculty of a university. Hence, the possible deterioration and abandonment of traditional methods of learning or dissemination of answers to questions, via lectures, via referring to books and periodicals (including encyclopedias), even data banks (which cannot begin to make all information available). Already "distance-learning" modalities make some learning and teaching patterns, such as lecturing in academia, highly anachronistic.

Yet, I believe that we cannot lose faith in exercising our right and competence in querying. I once wrote an editorial titled "A Preface to Inquiry" for the *Humanist*, which opened,

Why must Americans experience periodic birth pangs of awareness? Be challenged: "Wake up and see the Sputnik!" Be shocked, "Wake up and look at Watts!" [a Los Angeles ghetto] Be frightened: China just exploded her second nuclear weapon!" Be reassured: "Chins up, the Gross National Product has never been so high!" . . . Why?

Have we forgotten how to ask "Why" in our everlasting search for the "How"? Have we forgotten that curiosity is perhaps the first step to wisdom? Or is it not so much a matter of forgetting as of never having learned to ask? Have we perchance forfeited our constitutional guarantees of freedom by taking them for granted? Sacrificed them on the altar of fear? Have we ever really believed in free inquiry? Practiced it in our homes? At our jobs? In our communities? Even in our schools? And if it hasn't been practiced to its full extent, how much has this neglect eroded our human potential?[9]

I proceeded to fill two full pages with questions with nary a declarative sentence; yet, the editorial was filled with implications, innuendo, and suggestions; anger, too. And yet I recall no tide of response or rebuttal to my basic charges about the use of questions and the implication of their use as a basic tool. I even spoke of the Socratic flame and his catapulting Western civilization's philosophical inquiries into such basic questions as

What is justice?
What is love?
What is truth?

Now, while we use questions for getting through an average day, we do not manifest the skeptical doubts suggested by one state's favorite trademark, the citizen claiming to be from Missouri if s/he doubts. Yes, we've had some famous doubters, from Socrates to Mark Twain to Henry L. Mencken to Ellen Goodman and her op-ed columnist colleagues. Yet, how many know their works, or the periodical *Free Inquiry*?

And what about other modern societies? The French have a tradition and reputation of being skeptics. But are they? And what about the Germans, Chinese, Japanese, Kenyans, Australians, and the people of Bali? What difference does it make to us or to the world if they do or do not have similar traditions?

Theoretically, science is a worldwide phenomenon. Is querying? Is the use of the question? Can we apply the concept "half-life" to the process of querying to create a new spectrum of intensity ranging from the trivial to the significant to the eternal? For instance, most TV quiz shows and the board game Trivial Pursuit may be entertaining but do not add many dimensions to knowledge or curiosity, hence, what price do we pay as an evolving culture by spending so much time on such trivialization of human energy? Can this "numbing-out" process continue indefinitely? Could we perhaps spend more time in developing hierarchies of significance as part of curriculum development, with the focus on shaping and sharpening questions which will have lifelong significance rather than perpetuating bodies of knowledge which rapidly become obsolete, moment to moment in the ding-dang, clang-clang clamor of daily life?

Random Processes

It is fairly common knowledge that random sampling is a basic tool of science and the social sciences. By choosing "subjects," whether elements in nature or human beings and doing it randomly, presumably this eliminates the bias of making choices or collecting information based upon some preconceived notion. Hence it is built into the methodologies of the "pure scientist" and the political pollster. This is not to indulge in a complex analysis of its processes, outcomes, and reliability. Rather it is simply to describe a spoof that I employed, whimsically, when writing a twentieth-century history of my hometown, Saco, Maine. As I explained at the outset of a chapter called "Scrabble Interlude: A Phenomenological View of History":

This chapter of Saco history is comprised of disconnected twentieth-century events and situations chosen at random. In fact, I briefly recorded about 150 events on separate pieces of paper, put the slips of paper in a large brown supermarket paper bag, shook the bag well, then drew out the pieces and put them end to end as drawn from the bag. Only the reader can decide whether this approach to our history is more or less interesting, more or less real, more or less distorted than other methods. It may suggest one other thing; namely, that the ways of writing history are similar to the ways of living out one's three score and sixteen; there is variety and spice. Furthermore, my scrabble approach was a well-designed critique of those enamored with causal explanation of most events.[10]

I prefaced the chapter with a poem, "The Metaphor."

His was a Scrabble
view of history,
words and patterns
on an open board,
with random letters
&
events
swept
collectively
into musty dust bins
            sold
at Saturday morning garage sales,
a taker
            for ev'ry speck . . .

Self-Fulfilling and Self-Deceiving Prophecies

Among the many tools that scientists and other scholars include in their fundamental methodologies, I would include both of these prophecies. While inklings of such prophecies may have been inherent in previous conceptions and philosophies, Robert Merton, in 1949, wrote an insightful essay, "The Self-Fulfilling Prophecy." He focused upon the "moral alchemy" that in-groups use to denigrate out-group persons and behavior, even though both in-groups and out-groups manifest similar characteristics. Whereas, for instance, Abe Lincoln was a "cultural hero" embodying certain cardinal virtues, a Jew or black reflecting similar qualities could be perceived as "pushy," "crude," "beyond their place." In short, "the right activity by the wrong people becomes a thing of contempt, not of honor." Hence, self-fulfilling prophecy results in a metamorphosis or distortion of values, where achievements become faults and paradoxically enough virtues are shortcomings. As a result, powerful people continue to control and the passive frequently contribute to their own denigration.

As I state in a full analysis of this topic in *Free Inquiry*,[11] Merton observes at one point that "self-hypnosis through one's own propaganda is not an infrequent phase of the self-fulfilling prophecy," and therein lies my contention; namely, that the phenomenon of the self-fulfilling prophecy might in many instances be more accurately called "the self-deceiving prophecy!" In fact, we have come to associate "fulfillment" with the self-realization associated with humanistic psychology as evolved by Abraham Maslow, Carl Rogers, and their associates. This is an essentially positive concept; but as developed by Merton, "self-fulfilling" has dehumanizing connotations and denotations.

Those seeking a deeper analysis of this tool may easily locate my essay where I have provided several illustrations of self-deception. But let's look at one or two here: People may be so convinced that they can do nothing about a situation in a complex technological, urbanized, mechanized, televised, and bureaucratized society such as ours that they may deceive themselves into believing that they have no opportunity/power/right to protest, dissent, rise up in wrath to scream, "I object!" This is the kind of self-victimization that motivated men like Paolo Freire, Saul Alinsky, and other social-change activists to invent solutions in the name of justice, individual dignity, and equity.

I have closely watched the self-fulfilling prophecies metamorphosed into self-deceiving ones when new academic institutions have caved in to powerful accrediting agencies. Once the new group accepts the credentialing agency's power to ask out-of-order questions, they dignify the very answering process. As individuals our personal myths or habitual buying habits con us into purchasing goods and/or promises by advertisers, thus lulling us into self-deception. The huckster's line: "Buy Gismo No. 3 or Fad No. 5 and you'll achieve 'salvation'!" leads the potential buyer into self-deception. The logic goes, "It exists; therefore, I need it." Or the equally denigrating: "The community uses it as a yardstick; therefore, it shapes who I am." Or "What will people say?" Probably television and the Internet are the most insidious allies to self-deception in human history. We get the impression that we "can have it all"!

If you want to write a poem, haiku, song, social analysis, letter to the editor, choreograph a dance, try a new recipe (or invent one), whatever, but you find yourself *not* doing it, this is to suggest that you might deceive yourself into believing you can't, hence may *attempt* to explain your nonaction in terms of self-deception. In fact, you might devise an exercise for yourself which, using self-deception as a basic tool or explanation, paradoxically, may empower you to examine your failure to act.

Exercise No. 3: On Deception

- Draft a letter to the editor or the producer of a TV program regarding a product being advertised, e.g., a particular medication or toothbrush; issue a challenge that is clear about your own view of the product. Keep a copy of the letter so you may assess the recipient's response or nonresponse. Decide whether or not you wish to pursue the matter any further after you analyze whether or not the response is merely a matter of routine or form letter. Is it a put-down? Are you encouraged or discouraged?

- Make a list of occasions when you believe that you are being deceived by an outside agent. Make a similar list of the occasions when you may be deceiving yourself. Then attempt to "stand outside" yourself and distinguish between the two (or more) kinds of deception.

Now possessing a few useful tools, how can you discover how you learn best and use your brain, hands, controversial self, or even your age to an advantage? Also, with more and unique institutions encouraging lifelong learning (and even degree seeking), how can you ride on your learning curves and new opportunities to improve making a life as well as a living via creative processes?

Notes

1. Bertrand Russell, "New Dialogue," *New York Times Magazine* (December 16, 1951).
2. Andrew Macfarlane, letter, *Harper's* (February 1997): 4.

3. Eric Hoffer, *The True Believer* (New York: Harper, 1989). Whenever I use the term "true believer" in this volume, I use it in the sense that Hoffer uses it in his book: a person who rigidly believes that he has the truth!

4. Richard Dawson, *Chronicle of Higher Education* (November 29, 1996): A15.

5. Quoted in Neil Postman and Charles Weingartner, *Teaching as a Subversive Activity* (New York: Delacorte Press, 1969), p. 3.

6. Elyse N. Rapaport, *Creative Choices: Finding Meaning as Your Life Changes* (Fort Lauderdale, Fla.: Venture Press, 1996).

7. See Roy P. Fairfield, *Person-Centered Graduate Education* (Amherst, N.Y.: Prometheus Books, 1977), pp. 77–82.

8. Thurber, *Further Fables for Our Time* (any edition).

9 Roy P. Fairfield, "A Preface to Inquiry," *Humanist* 27, no. 1 (1967): 3–4.

10. Roy P. Fairfield, *New Compass Points* (Saco, Maine: Bastille Books, 1988), pp. 90–95.

11. Roy P. Fairfield, "The Self-Deceiving Prophecy," *Free Inquiry* 6, no. 1 (1985/86): 56–57.

CHAPTER 3

Learning Styles

What Is Learning?

In the twentieth century there probably have been enough pages written about learning to pave an interstate highway between the east and west coasts! The process has been treated conceptually, empirically, situationally, institutionally, existentially, politically, and beyond, for it is, indeed, central to human survival. Even as we read or reread this, neurophysiologists are discovering and plotting the quadrillions of paths in the brain wherein we store knowledge and transmit it from one sector of the brain and body to another.[1] The potential for unique combinations is so astronomical, it is painful to hear or read about human beings who insist upon limiting their understanding in one or even a thousand ways. Each of us encounters the "universe" of nature, of human devising, or of social composition in billions of ways each day, week, month, year, decade, lifetime. Hence, to diminish the quality or quantity of such "encounters" is to destroy human potential. It is my contention that learning, no matter its content, must enhance both quality and quantity of thought, action, health, etc. Hence, my lifetime battle with willful ignorance and my advocacy of exploring a cluster of questions;

namely, How do you learn best? When? Where? Why? and possibly, With whom? And how do they relate to creative processes?

It is a paradox of enormous proportion to realize that for all of the twentieth-century studies of learning and for all that we have learned, there are still two paramount methods used by professional educators in the context of two basic paradigms whether those who are presumably learning are eight months or eighty years of age: didactic (or telling) and hands-on (or learning by *do*-ing). And of these two probably the didactic takes precedence in most schooling situations. Again, many studies have been done of the two phenomena. Marilyn Ferguson, an educator and social philosopher, contrasts the two rather succinctly in her *Aquarian Conspiracy*; this is a summary of her summary:

Assumptions re: Old Paradigm	Assumptions re: the New
Emphasis on content	Emphasis on learning how to learn, ask questions, with the stress on content
Product	Process
Rigid structure	Flexibility
Divergent thinking discouraged	Whole-brain approach
Labeling contributes structure	Avoid labeling

Those wishing a full outline of these two paradigms may wish to consult Ferguson's brilliant analysis. Those wishing to focus on experiential learning for children will benefit enormously by reading Maria Montessori's *Spontaneous Activity in Education*, the first of three volumes dealing with her "Advanced Method." Equally important, perhaps, would be to find a local Montessori school and visit in order to get a firsthand appreciation of her methods and the excitement that they generate.[2]

When dealing with large numbers of people (as in a democratic society wherein "everybody" presumably can participate in the process), no doubt it is *easier* to expound the "truth" from a podium, lectern, pulpit, etc., or via video, camera, projector, and microphone; in short, assume that the "receiver" is astute enough, is prepared to absorb this "truth" if his posterior is strong enough and his brain is like a blackboard. And, of course, in a classroom or TV or computer course the self-fulfilling (or self-deceiving) prophecy is in full operation because the students (whether "learners" or not) are there with their notebooks to record, as best they can, what the dispenser is mouthing about. Then, too, the power structure is in full view: a spiritual guide, no matter the denomination or sect, is in a position to describe/prescribe the sanctions for "not getting it"; in the classroom at any level, the teacher (whether a facilitator of learning or not) can dish out the grades in the context of general rules prescribed by the school, the profession, the community standards (high or low). I believe that this does not overgeneralize or simplify the reality in this moment of our national life even though a new factor such as "virtual reality" is a ubiquitous force as we move from an era of print literacy to the era of electronic or graphic consumption and presumed literacy. Above all, this didactic system, which calls for a particular style of learning, begins with the assumption that somebody or somebodies have the *truth* and are prepared to dispense it. Equally prepared is an entire industry of evaluators: test-makers such as those who construct SATs; accreditation groups (to check the checkers); professional associations who presumably set state, regional, and national standards. Actually, it is only fair to observe that such evaluators actually do not care how persons or groups learn so long as they can pass the official tests; but it should be noted that the self-deceiving prophecy is in full operation. Fulfillment is more probable if one follows the rules and these are established by—the Establishment! Hence perpetuate illusions about quality, standards, and so on. In a credentials-happy society, it *seems* that the externals count most! In contrast, not everybody is fooled. To cite Hamlet when confronted with the "reality" of seems and responding to his mother's observations, he said, "Seems, madam! Nay, it is: madam; I know not 'seems.' "³

It is tempting for a skeptic, such as myself, to dichotomize this issue and argue that hands-on or experiential learning is more valuable than that achieved via didactic modalities. Since the rise and fall of the American philosopher John Dewey during the first half of the twentieth century, many have been inclined to promote such dichotomizing. I must confess that I more or less "made it," kindergarten through doctorate, via exploitation of the didactic method. I followed the leadership of my teachers and professors, was bright enough to understand the symbols and politics of it (whether assessing what my parents, community, or profession demanded), took "good notes," memorized what I had to, fulfilled that learning which enabled me to pass the tests, graduated from class to class, degree to degree. Luckily I had a fairly good retentive memory *in the moment*. But upon reading Canadian humorist Stephen Leacock's definition of a college education as that which you have left over after you've forgotten all you ever learned, I came to question my own memory and the "mammon" it had served for twenty-three school years. But my "enlightenment" did not arrive simply via the proverbial "road to Damascus." Hard reflection led to many insightful flashbacks.

When I was a boy my father "taught" better than he was aware. He frequently pointed to an automobile in his public garage, a car he'd agreed to repair, and would say to me, "Roy, drop the crankcase on that Buick, take off the cylinder head, and pull the connecting rods and valves." Obedient son that I was (most of the time!), I would select appropriate wrenches and go to work in the oil, grease, and dirt. Perhaps my biggest lesson came when I was a freshman in high school. Dad put me to work on the Buick with orders just quoted. I struggled almost an hour trying to "drop the crankcase," but I failed because the case would not clear the tie-rods that coordinated the front wheels on cars of that era. After whining a bit (he would not permit profanity!), I went back to him as he worked under another car and reported that I "couldn't do it." He would rarely take "no" or "I can't" for an answer. He looked up at me from his awkward position and issued his challenge, saying, "Look! If you can't take the crankcase off the engine, take the engine off the crankcase!" That set me to thinking and I did, indeed, change my angle of vision and got the crankcase off by removing the radiator, the tie-rods, anything else in my way. Imagine my delight two decades later in reading John Dewey's writing as well as Alfred North Whitehead's *Science in the Modern World* to hear them advocate *changing the problem* if you can't solve it. With 20/20 hindsight I put many another chore that my parents proposed into that context; they usually shoved tool or task into my hands to let me learn by doing. At eighteen almost single-handedly I did the carpentry that nearly doubled the size of our family home. Also, I worked seventy-two months in industry, learning essentially the same way.

In short, in school I learned mostly via didactic means, but in tandem situations I also came to cherish the hands-on, discovery method. It became easier, as an evolving methodologist, to see the virtues and disadvantages of each. And while I participated in essentially the didactic (so-called lecture) system for seventeen years of "teaching" in traditional settings (Bates College, Athens College, Hofstra University, Ohio University), I became increasingly disaffected with it. Despite the overwhelming odds against motivating large classes (ranging from a low of twenty to highs in the hundreds), I attempted to combine the two methods wherever feasible; in short, *making assignments* (note the *assumption* and *implications* in those two words) that would virtually force students to discover as much as possible for themselves. I also became increasingly critical of *all* methods done in the name of discovery which, indeed made *assumptions* about who has the power to make assignments, who has the corner on the market of "truth." Also I learned that each "truth" has its own methodology for determining "fact" (cf. chapter 2).

Today I would argue that some fields of endeavor (possibly mathematics?) *may* require more teacher-professorial direction than experiential discovery. Yet, I would also contend that the very system which presumes to elicit "truth" may, indeed, serve as a prophylactic against achieving it. The sad, if not tragic, fact remains: many forces (including power structures, community myths, tenure practices, etc.) tend to block those who *do* believe in and know how to encourage experiential learning. Also, those teachers at any level who persist in "pushing the river" and/or "swimming against the tide" risk burnout when dealing with so many students in the straitjackets of "quarter, semester, grading periods, courses." Even self-discovery processes require some kind of reporting. The system demands it. Reports require reading, usually in a time frame. Colearners, teachers, facilitators—call them what one will—risk their sanity, to say nothing about other aspects of their lives, by following their beliefs. Work-study programs, on-the-job training, and other such combining of didactic and experiential learning alleviate some of the sterility of learning modalities; yet, I do not hear enough persons in a wide enough context asking, *how do you* or *I learn best?*

(More later in this chapter about other modalities, including distance learning and the Internet.)

Learning as a Subversive Activity

Throughout human history there is much evidence of discouraging learning because it is probably a subversive activity. If elders in ancient Chinese culture were honored, then it ill became youngsters to challenge their knowledge. In nonliterate cultures, again, those who lived longest were most honored and were "keepers of the flame." And by limiting who might join the tribal council, whatever its form, the culture's continuity demanded control of knowledge. In some instances, as in ancient Greece, "citizenship" was very limited in the so-called Athenian democracy. While we honor the memory of Socrates and his questioning techniques, surely those in power could not be very enthusiastic about his walking around the agora or streets of Athens, asking questions and making enemies as some modern observers have noted. Hence, no wonder that the un-Athenian Activities Committee made him drink the hemlock.

Logically enough, if learning is subversive, teaching is more so.[4] Western civilization has had its share of those who deemed learning as a subversive activity. The established church, with its catechisms, papal doctrines, inquisitions, and hierarchical structures is a story in itself about the ways in which power and knowledge-by-imprimatur perpetuated themselves by controlling what their members might believe and know, and how they should think. When people wanted to defy this control, they faced the threat of spending eternity in the kind of vivid hell that Dante describes in his *Divine Comedy*. Church builders also incorporated the threat in their gargoyles, and many painters depicted it in their vast numbers of canvases. While it might not be stated overtly that learning is always subversive, it was certainly inferred.

Also, the crowned heads of western Europe, using every conceivable weapon against those who would challenge their power, surely did not encourage learning in any democratic sense. While Oxford might have been founded shortly after the invasion of the Normans, what percentage of Englishmen ever enrolled? What methods of learning prevailed century after century? What is the essential mode of learning today? Former colonial nations, in Africa for instance, still pay for Europeans having controlled via contrived ignorance during colonial rule. This is demonstrated poignantly in Barbara Kingsolver's novel, *The Poisonwood Bible*.[5] The family she depicts is doomed to fail when pitting its biblical tradition against tribal wisdom.

Our own history is not above reproach. It was dangerous for slaves in the American South to become literate. And until relatively recently, most American women were systematically confined to the home, with far too large a percentage of males doing everything possible to keep them "barefoot, pregnant, and in the kitchen." Female schooling was confined to elite "finishing schools." Only during the past half century has the "playing field" been "leveled," both academically and in athletics. While in general women now have more opportunities, there are still pockets of ideology and geography wherein women are thought to be "inferior," hence given little opportunity to advance via learning. The glass ceiling is no figment of their imagination. And some families with limited funds will afford opportunities for their sons but not their daughters. In some instances with which I am familiar, institutional policies, family legend, and mythology about females dictate such decisions. Too frequently, the argument runs, "After all, she's going to get married and/or pregnant, why invest more money in her education?" Encouraging, however, is the fact that many more young women seem to defy such arguments; also, with more lifelong learning opportunities available today, they can "go back to school" even if family circumstances dictate a break in formal learning sequences.

One may facetiously describe Western philosophy as "massive verbal retaliation."[6] Whether Aristotle was taking on Plato . . . *or* Roger Bacon challenging Aquinas . . . *or* Immanuel Kant opposing David Hume. Even to this day schools of thought such as the pragmatic take on the idealists, the realists challenge the existentialists. Despite pledges to be ecumenical, university departments play power games to decide emphasis. In most instances advocates of the "truth" in each argue interminably and sometimes incoherently, at least for the so-called average citizen. They sometimes charge one another with being ignorant and develop power structures in the academic world to prove who's right and who's wrong! The "right" is usually the stronger or the one with the most funds.

At a more practical level, political theorists have argued that those in the other camp *are* ignorant! and their views subversive. Probably the most important conflict over that issue in modern times grew out of the Russian revolution and its counterparts throughout the world. Surely, for seven decades the Russian regime stifled debate regarding ideologies other than Marxist-Leninist ones. A state apparatus of universities, following Marxist-Leninist theories, kept strict control of learning, publication, and the "culture" of scientific advance. And the Russian inferno, contrary to Dante's, included time in Siberia or the Gulag. Aleksandr I. Solzhenitsyn's books delineate those "circles" of Siberia as vividly and powerfully as Dante's. Few of today's adults in the United States can be unaware of that complex of realities that made any non-Communist position suspect in the Soviet Union.

The other side of that coin, of course, is the fact that in most quadrants it was perceived or inferred to be subversive if one were a Communist in the United States. At its nadir, simply to be told that you might be on one of Sen. Joseph McCarthy's infamous lists of American Communists was threatening and potentially dangerous, hence subversive. While the Soviet Union has been dismantled, it is probably still perceived by many to be subversive to advocate a Marxist position in the United States although the so-called New Left has risen and fallen in recent years, mostly in the context of academic freedom, another long and contentious battle filled with both villains and heroes.

It is probably safe to say that any "true believer," whether a dyed-in-the-wool ideologist from one place on the political spectrum (right-left, up-down, over-beyond), or in any other direction, is a potential subversive. After all, she knows that she is "right." It's the position that makes "political correctness" and "ethnic cleansing" so dangerous. Our faith in democratic processes, whether majority-minority rule, due process, consensus building, or separation of powers, looks intellectually "mushy" when perceived from a hard ideological position. But ironically enough, the net result may confirm French social theorist Jean-Jacques Rousseau's belief in the "general will"! Or it may affirm the insights that James Madison reflected in that famous "Number Ten" *Federalist Paper* (1787) which argued that the "dire effect of factions" could be negated by a governmental structure allowing them to rub the thorns off one another.

It seems safe to generalize that "freedom is frightening."[7] And as journalist A. J. Liebling once observed, "Freedom of the press is guaranteed only to those who own one."[8] This is not too different from the observation that whoever controls the mimeograph machine or computer controls the revolution.

Let us now consider the computer and its place in the democratization of learning and communication.

Distance Learning and the Internet

It's neither fair nor accurate to think of "distance learning" as being a wholly new vehicle of learning. Not only have books been used "at a distance" from their origins, but also think of the number of famous letter writers who made use of that process; for example, Thomas Jefferson and John Adams exchanging letters and ideas for nearly half a century. In a sense, correspondence courses are viable learning modalities and a logical extension of private letter writing, *except*: such courses are formalized, systematized, and carefully controlled by institutions and their authoritative representatives who control the interchange with students located in some distant place.

And what about technology in a wired society! Think of phone conversations through which you have learned about family, business opportunities, and travel vistas. In recent years, radio, television, computer, and audiovisual "revolutions" really do constitute a global "classroom." What *is* new is the recognition in some (but not all) educational quadrants that learning via these new revolutionary means can be as legitimate as formal learning modalities. Television courses, even on the networks, are now old hat. Likewise television is a way to reach larger groups who may be unable to squeeze into an auditorium: teleconferencing in corporate, medical, legal, and educational settings is commonplace.

Another stage of distance learning came into being in the late 1960s and early 1970s when Samuel Baskin, an Antioch professor who had been immersed in Antioch's fifty-year-old work-study program, dreamed up the concept of a "university without walls" (UWW). With aid from the U.S. Office of Education, Ford and Kresge Foundation funds, Sam and Goodwin Watson implemented and coordinated a variety of such programs through a consortial network, the Union for Experimenting Colleges and Universities. That consortium reached its peak in the mid-1970s before each of the cooperating institutions absorbed such UWW programs as live options and/or abandoned them. Malls Without Walls, a catch-phrase of Market America, is no doubt a variation on a theme! Likewise, a tangle of e-purchasing outlets with their "come-ons."

Meanwhile, Goodwin and I launched the doctoral UWW program in 1970. Although we had no grants for the start-up, we did have institutional support from persons such as Drs. James Dixon and Royce Pitkin, presidents of Antioch and Goddard Colleges, as well as other presidents of the consortium. This, too, was a distance-learning program in which learners were linked into a committee comprised of experts in the students' field of study as well as union peers. Also each participant was encouraged to enjoin the recommended process which encouraged the learner to chair her committee and evolve a learning contract, hence was person-centered. For the most part the network of trust and support that we created worked. Learners enrolled in the program engaged with their committees; it was long on learning contracts and short on "courses." At its best the Union Graduate School (UGS) encouraged self-empowerment, exploration into all of the resources (human and material) which existed "out there somewhere." At its best we encouraged learners to explore options to find their best learning mode as well as relevant bodies of knowledge. At its best we convinced our learners that "the process is the product." Many were encouraged to unbelievable creativity. The UGS story is well documented elsewhere in my *Person-Centered Graduate Education*[9] and the union's periodical, *Network*. This is simply to emphasize the fact that the learning took place by trust, in curiosity, freedom to learn, and strong motivation—and a modicum of didactics. Our learners and their colearners (the faculty) created and utilized a network that became recognized as a viable learning resource long before the "Internet" became a common household word and Macintosh and "PC" computer realities. UGS learners and faculty were scattered to the wind but used every manner of communication to join in learning objectives.

The Union Graduate School was not alone in pioneering distance learning. Other schools such as Walden, Fielding, Saybrook, and Capella have designed variations on the distance-learning theme. But it is instructive to observe that almost every institution of this type, including Union Institute, in the name of quality control has caved in to pressures from the powerful regional accrediting associations. These pressuring forces, still traditional and very much in the hands of various establishments, are, almost by definition, designed to encourage pouring learning into preordained "boxes" in the mind. In other words, distance learning is fine so long as it's "con-fined." And such confinement tends to be determined by the traditional disciplines (English, psychology, physics, etc.) or by corporate expectations (the bottom line), or by other credentialing criteria (how many faculty Ph.D.s from accredited institutions? quality and quantity of publications? library access?), and so on. In many instances, it is clear that both accreditors and the caved-in administrators of so-called nontraditional institutions *start* with their conclusions, despite claims of empirical integrity. In one instance that I experienced firsthand, I heard a college president disclaim that his institution was nontraditional after months and months of advertising to the contrary. He had "sold out" to the accreditors; yet denied that, too. It is no wonder that a distinguished administrator in a well-known midwestern university agrees with me that one word tends to characterize much of university life— "mendacity." He sometimes translates that rather dignified and complex concept into a street-smart description: "Bull——!" It is not too far-fetched to claim that such instances illustrate how hard some persons and institutions fight "to make the world safe for hypocrisy" (with a verbal assist to Woodrow Wilson!).

In short, such forces are short on trust in learners learning but insistent upon the boxes, calling them "courses," "knowledge modules," "curriculum adaptations," "time-serving," or whatever. This also tends to be the case for undergraduate UWW's although the alert and innovative learner can usually find some "wiggle room" to pursue her interests, despite the credentialing society in which we live. But, freedom to inquire is, indeed, scary for those encumbered by conventional wisdoms (wizard and "whiz-dumbs"?).

Linking with the Internet

By this time in our cultural development, it's a rare person owning a computer or aspiring to own one who doesn't perceive the Internet as a vast complex of entangled wires, fiber optics, and information that now embraces the world. Anybody owning a computer and the appropriate software from the organizations serving that consumer can tap into virtually every pocket of knowledge on the earth. And if not the knowledge itself, the vital unanswered questions which humankind has programmed into the network. In some instances, too, knowledge and/or data for which the questions have not yet been asked (My favorite question, even of so-called knowledgeables: "What is your favorite *un*asked question?"). (See chapter 5.)

But the major objection of the traditionalist, working with the neophyte learner (and most learners are neophytes in the minds of a "true-believer"), is fairly simple: most of the knowledge "out there somewhere" on the Internet is not systematized in terms of preestablished "courses" of institutionalized curriculums at *any* level although the number of courses is increasing astronomically. So, they ask, "How can you expect learners to go 'out there' to find appropriate information without guidance?" In fact, is there really a there there? Hence, the standard procedure is to guarantee that knowledge is delivered (packaged/boxed) in terms of courses in curriculums. Some little piece of that package may require a modicum of learner ingenuity to put the puzzle together; but surely, the traditionalist continues, if institutions are to keep their accreditation, their prestige, their control by faculties, deans, provosts, and others in the academic hierarchy, they must not be vulnerable to charges of "sloppiness," "lack of standards," "poor quality," etc. In short, even with the Internet available (perhaps *because* it's available?), it may undermine the "knowledge industry." In short, it is probably subversive! Surely, the Internet itself is uncontrollable, except in economic terms when it comes to accessibility. It is instructive to note, however, that degree-seeking *is* controllable.

Kent State University attempts to redefine distance learning by calling it "Distributive Learning."[10] The sad thing is: while the school "aspires to become an active leader in the implementation and use of technological infrastructures" and serve people who are "placebound," it echoes what goes on in the classroom and does not avoid the criticism of keen observers who call what's happening for what it is; namely, "more of same," whether by correspondence courses or carefully controlled curriculum. This is hardly learner-directed as defined by the Union Graduate School when creating academic committees. While it is doubtful that any institution will be able to control access to the network (even when they require that their enrollees own a computer), it is fairly safe to assume that the Internet is a threat to the existence of traditional institutions . . . *unless* distance learning can somehow be confined to curriculum boxes or receive some kind of imprimatur from prestigious institutions such as Harvard or Stanford. Likewise, e-mail is a threat to the future of the U.S. Post Office, especially as ownership of computers is further democratized and despite the sale of postage stamps via the Internet. Distance learning may be the wave of the future, but it's possible that traditional institutions will not realize this until they cease to exist, functionally at least!

Objectivity versus Subjectivity?

During the twentieth century, empirical research expanded from the natural sciences into the social sciences and onward into the arts, presumably with one major goal: to achieve "objectivity." Such a widening of application has had some unfortunate consequences to accompany the positive results. While the process has no doubt led to the accumulation of Himalayas of verifiable substantial, practical data, it has also led to irrelevant, picayune, and abstract "information" which is next to worthless. Alfred North Whitehead, the great philosopher, deemed the result as the "Fallacy of Misplaced Concreteness."[11] Translate: "taking data out of context" or similar to the spirit of William Wordsworth's view of science; namely, "We murder only to dissect."[12] The implications for learning have been dire especially when the acceleration of the accumulation of data makes it both impossible and unnecessary for anybody to "learn it all" since we have easy access to that information via computer.

Researchers and hence teachers have made human beings "subjects" and/or "objects" in the name of objectivity. Presumably this has been done to eliminate bias or the "sin" of "subjectivity." Hence, a vast literature on methodology of doing research, with its implications for teachers and learning, to avoid those biases that lead to erroneous results. Growing from this, of course, has been a multitude of administrative rules, regulations, and procedures to avoid the *appearance* of a bias which might leave one open to legal suit, subject an institution to court rulings, leave one vulnerable to criticism and charges of fraud, and so on. Literature growing out of these procedures is saturated with the impersonal words "the subject," or other such designations. As might be expected, such literature denigrates feeling and/or personal references; in short, it is mostly abstract and minimizes human content. It counteracts the views of contemporary philosopher Michael Polanyi, and his discoveries about the integrity of "personal knowing." This is all very fine for some topics such as demography and other social topics or issues where data can, indeed, be collected, manipulated, and summarized. It can be demoralizing for those concerned for the juices of human experience. One tragic result of this trend toward so-called objective research and teaching is: those who control academia politically tend to control the methodology. Except in the past decade or so, when alternative methodologies have become acceptable, simply to use the term "research" implied an empirical approach.[13] Fortunately, fads and/or perspectives in academia often come and go as frequently and inexplicably as they do in the world of fashion though perhaps with less volatility. Pressures against nonempirical research (frequently any topic that can't be reduced to numbers) have led to counterpressures from those who advocate phenomenological approaches. In short, the study of humans in the process of becoming aware as in "personal knowing." Hence, qualitative research has been coming into its own. In one sense, I find Einstein's comment about imagination symbolic. He once declared, "Imagination is more important than knowledge." Note that "more important" does not exclude the study of and search for knowledge. So my own "battle cry" is symbolized in my oft-spoken comment to learners with whom I've worked; namely, "It's okay to say 'I.'" This is especially important when they are inclined to refer to themselves in the third person or use the term "subjects" when they are speaking about individual persons who breathe, bleed, and speak.

Amazingly enough, it has not been easy to convince some academics that alternative methods, both scholarly and legitimate, do exist. But the impact of humanistic psychology, an increasing acceptance of journaling in its many forms, and other introspective modalities all have contributed to processes which most literary folk, novelists, dramatists, and poets have known "forever"! It's fine to write from the heart or to listen to one's own muse. This is not to denigrate genuine efforts to work toward objectivity. But it is to discount efforts to apply it universally. I sometimes am forced by situation to give credence to the matter by facetiously observing, "Objectivity is what I say it is!"[14] (Wasn't it Oliver Wendell Holmes who said that the U.S. Constitution is what the Supreme Court said it was?)

Of course, it may be equally entrapping and potentially nonconducive to a learning atmosphere if a person is forced to follow *any* one method to its logical and/or illogical conclusion, unless that person is curious and does it as another exercise in methodology and/or learning to discover still another alternative to learning. Again, we may be reminded of Bertrand Russell's "New Decalogue," one commandment of which runs, "Have no respect for the authority of others, for there are always contrary authorities to be found."[15]

Theory and Practice

As recounted above, I grew up in a family that believed in practical, hands-on learning. If you wanted a boy to learn about carpentry or a girl to learn about sewing, you encouraged them to pick up a hammer and saw, thread a needle, or pedal a sewing machine. In fact, if any extreme existed, my parents, neighbors, and friends were part of the vein of American anti-intellectualism that tended to downgrade "book learning" except what one learned *for* the teacher in school. Schooling, yes, but not too much or too far! I doubt if they ever saw the contradiction in those views. And yet, other factors were in play; namely, appreciation of the apprenticeship system in the trades, learning by everyday *doing.* So, if we made practical mistakes, that was part of "paying your dues." Most middle-class persons felt the reinforcing cultural pressures upon them, encouraging "manual training" and "domestic science" in the elementary schools. Also, local industry and trade guilds were proven ways to integrate the town's youth into the workplace, even during the Great Depression. Pursued upon graduation from high school, such programs were frequently referred to as "the College of Hard Knocks."

Meanwhile in the larger world: beginning with the University of Cincinnati and Antioch in the early 1920s, colleges and universities have evolved work-studies programs on a large scale, using a variety of configurations. The belief has been tested at both secondary and higher education levels; namely that learners learn best if they can combine studies and hands-on experience; some institutions structure this process in alternate semesters or quarters; some do both concurrently or in parallel modes. It is difficult to quantify this phenomenon because it changes so rapidly; but a large percentage of institutions feature the process as an integral part of their curriculum. During the past half century an increasing number of high schools have adopted similar systems. It is probably a logical consequence of the American tendency to be practical, even expedient, while experimenting with new modes of learning. Also, the work-study phenomenon has been a source of income for learners at every level as well as a source of person power to do work that might not otherwise get done, in developing environmental themes, in fulfilling socially desirable processes such as staffing nursing homes or evolving library and computer facilities. Work-study money comes from both public and private sectors.

Less tangible but no less significant, emphasis on work-study relates to improving learners' self-concepts, especially focusing upon self-empowerment. A successful stint of work may reinforce success in the classroom; yet, even if one or the other do not reinforce one another, experience is certainly invaluable even if it teaches learners negative results. It can be a stepping stone to later careers.

When we constructed the Ph.D. program of the Union Graduate School (UGS) in 1970 and were determined to combine theory and practice, we incorporated an "internship" requirement. It required several years to expand the concept and guidelines beyond the medical model. Eventually, it was to include various kinds of opportunity, including the apprenticeship notion; a neophyte poet might understudy with a poet, likewise a would-be academic administrator or would-be corporate officer. We encouraged those aspiring to teach to find a class to teach as well as a "supervisor" or facilitator. Many in the corporate world were encouraged "to turn their jobs upside down" or find another whose nature related more meaningfully to their scratch pad, spend a significant amount of time at the newly configured work situation, and have it verified by a responsible person. One simply could not "do business as usual" and call it an internship. Running parallel to that expectation was the requirement that enrollees would take whatever steps (journaling, photographing, etc.) necessary to document their experiences as well as enable them to write a reflective "essay" on personal growth, describing how their internship affected the more intellectual dimensions of their programs. What insights did it afford? To which body of literature did it lead? How did they combine theory and practice? Historically, graduate work has been long on the intellectual and short on the experiential or affective dimensions of learning . . . except insofar as teachers have engaged in classroom activity or institutions such as professional schools of art, design, business, engineering, and law have required hands-on experience. Few have done much about "personal growth" and reflection.

It seems fair to conclude that work-study enhances both social and individual development, hence most institutions continue to employ it when establishing curriculums and/or learning modalities. My major criticism is this: it sometimes promises more than it can possibly deliver. Supervisors of such programs are frequently denigrated as less capable than "regular" classroom teachers. Also, unfortunately, campus coordinators do not have enough time to visit the learner and her supervisor on the job or discuss the learner's experience in depth, either on location in seminars or interviews back on campus. The individual learners as well as those in groups may write papers about the value of their experiences, but the integration of work and study seems only partially achieved. Possibly such integration is too much of an ideal, a "consummation devoutly to be wished."

To Saw a Board

Perhaps a logical outcome of my personal experience of combining theory and practice is writing about it. I've had several in-depth dialogues with doctoral candidates regarding the topic. One woman from India urged me to write a piece, "The Dignity of Hands,"[16] which she could share with her associates in the Madras region as a way of enabling dialogue with Indian students and colleagues ("intellectuals") who tend to denigrate the use of the hands in doing work, a cultural attitude she wished to counter. Another article, "To Saw a Board,"[17] incorporated a letter exchange with a former Peace Corps volunteer on the topic when he requested tuition rebates to pay for "a backsaw, fine and rough crosscut, C-clamps, auger and bits" to complete his project. In a standard doctoral context, I might have been turned off by his request, but he went on to explain that "becoming familiar with carpentry skills is part of my program in education-psychology. I feel it is—probably most importantly—working with my hands; also I want to learn for myself what Phien knew" (a figure from Chinese history). Mark closed his letter by citing a metaphor I had shared with my student and faculty colleagues some months before; namely,

Do we sweat
with adze and chisel
to whittle spokes
for an oval wheel?

In short, I departed from traditional doctoral advising when engaging in such dialogues, to encourage experimenting with experiential connections.

To dramatize and reinforce my viewpoints: I began one of our Union Graduate School colloquia, fortunately enough, held near my home workshop, by starting the session in a dormitory common room by dragging a "bushel" of tools before the assembly of new matriculants. Since this was their first encounter with me and I with them, they could have no preconceived ideas of what I might do. I set up a sawhorse; brought in a substantial plank; set up an even heavier piece of dimension material; unpacked hammers, chisels, planes, etc., as well as my chain saw in a histrionic manner. And for the next hour I not only demonstrated the use of such tools but (taking essential precautions and instructions) thrust both the chain saw and other tools into the hands of both men and women, encouraging them to hammer nails and slice off pieces of the plank. Some were reluctant to enjoin such a new experience; some began asking the "Why?" of such demonstrations. All seemed to enjoy and remember; for, even today, two decades following those events, some of the UGS graduates write to remind me of that episode and its meaning. Also, we talked so much about journaling/logging in that group that two of the fellows carried a rather heavy pulpwood log from the banks of the nearby river to the meeting room and placed it on the middle of the carpet. In a day or three, after the surface of the log had dried, most of the members of the group kneeled or lay on the floor beside that log to scribble their names, draw pictures, or make other inscriptions. Among the most amusing: a row of ants that emerged from the log through a knothole, traveled along the log's surface, and then disappeared into another imperfection in the wood! I salvaged this artifact and occasionally take it out of storage as a reminder of my efforts to heighten those learners' awareness and to encourage use of both head and hands in their doctoral programs.

One final illustration of the creative potential from such an interaction: since 1970 I have had ongoing correspondence and face-to-face dialogues with Craig Mosher, a UGS graduate, about this topic. We have exchanged books, articles, and newspaper clippings, and speculated on values growing from integrating ideas and theories. Upon one recent occasion, we spent three days together reconstructing the shutters for our oceanside cottage, ever vulnerable to high water and winds. Whenever I install those shutters today, I think of those re-FIRE-ing three hot summer days of conversation and the net result of our joint effort. As an additional bonus, he asked me to teach him how to write haiku. We sat at our kitchen table, for a time writing alternate lines of that three-line challenge in the mode suggested by my Do-It-Yourself Hiaku Kit. This began another exchange of sharing seaside haiku and those inspired by his living and traveling in the Midwest. Also together we explored a part of the Everglades, rich in alligators and cormorants, writing and sharing haiku as we explored. In many ways, too, we share in what Chris Cernich in *Newsweek* called, "The Romance of Old Tools," in which he claims that "Tools help us fashion the physical world into a place where we want to live."[18] Furthermore, this vein of interest continues my boyhood use of tools, when I served as a tool coordinator in a textile machine shop for a few years during World War II, and more recently in compiling the book *Humanizing the Workplace*.[19]

Exercise No. 4: Handling Tools

Since there are some situations where familiarity does *not* breed contempt, it might be the better part of valor to take a few steps to learn about tools you've never had in your hands:

1. Ask a friend with a workshop to introduce you to several tools you've never used, and let you practice using them.
2. Take apart some simple device you have in your home, then put it back together; if you have pieces left over, you can get help salvaging them and/or join our "throw-away society" and toss them, too! Be daring!

3. If you've not become acquainted with the motor in your car, have somebody introduce you to it; remove a piece or two, then learn how they contribute to the car's operation.

4. If you live close to any museum that features tool collections, go to the museum with a focused intention of inspecting tools you've never seen before. No doubt a museum docent or attendant will not only show you how they work, but also discuss their importance in the history of carpentry, cabinetmaking, or toolmaking. If you live near or have the opportunity to visit the Shelburne, Vermont, Museum of Americana, you could easily spend a full day there becoming acquainted with the vast variety of tools that it has on display.

An important principle: have a hands-on experience and put it into social and historical context.

Learning in the Marketplace

This is a variation on a theme. For decades alert teachers from kindergarten through the doctoral level have encouraged observation in the marketplace. When formalized for a given class, it was probably called a "field trip." Both teachers and students have sharpened their powers of using all of their senses by way of visiting museums, factories, stores, malls, theaters, symphonies, mines, you name it! Such field trips usually involve both planning and follow-up, hence giving students experience in organization and the "realities" of money, legal implications of such trips, and importance of social behavior. They also feature discussion, question-and-answer interface with those visited, as well as follow-up reaction papers and further explorations back in the classroom. Usually, too, both teachers and students enjoy the change of scenery and learning modalities.

Increasingly, too, teachers in every field and adult programs such as Elderhostel bring current social and political issues (e.g., war, crime, peace, etc.), mathematical problems, environmental perspectives, and so on into the classroom or communications center. Both improved technological facilities bring video, television, and computers as close as a classroom switch, and they do it so much more reliably and imaginatively than they did only a decade or so ago. Yet school administrators and teachers are under heavy pressure from parents to censor content which only a few such parents regard as "undesirable." Such problems may eventually be "taken all the way to the Supreme Court." Libraries, too, have become "communications centers." Indeed, the marketplace is no longer "out there" in the remote somewhere or in the void, an abstraction. And when it comes to the esoteric nature of the stock market, for instance, a teacher merely has to tune in to Wall Street, graphically, verbally, conceptually, intellectually. And when a major event occurs on the world stage, "current event" may translate into "simultaneous event" if the television is "properly used" to bring news to the classroom. CNN and most of the other networks have, indeed, developed the earth's peoples into a "global village." Videotape and simulcast has made it possible to make graphic the realities of the variety of the world's cultures; today's students can learn by sitting at the United Nations council tables. None of this is automatic or necessarily produces universal perspectives; different learners will see "different" images on the same screen; yet, the potential is enormous, especially when employed by well-informed and imaginative teachers, at every level. In such instances the teacher no longer needs to be a perambulating encyclopedia; rather, she becomes a facilitator of learning, a much more complicated and demanding job than the classical (and probably stereotypical) role. Such teachers may easily burn themselves out when *their* learning must continue at the same pace as their learners or the rate of change is exponential, not simply arithmetical; it's a role about which parents, educational power brokers, and the general citizenry must learn, reassess, and appreciate. Failure to do so will drive the most effective from the profession.

Aging with Dignity

For some strange reason, political, social, and economic organizations are waking up to the fact that people are living longer! Where they've had their heads (in the sand?), I do not know. Sure, we've had gerontological studies, academic programs, senior focusing on a variety of topics, etc. Crises in Medicare and Social Security have no doubt been learning experiences for many segments of the population. But many stereotypes regarding older persons' habits, learning capacities, and the very nature of longevity itself are being challenged—all of which have implications for learning. Even the American Association of Retired Persons (AARP) is beginning to think of persons between the ages of fifty and one hundred ten as seniors *learning*.

While there is a growing literature pertaining to aging, this is to encourage any newcomer to awareness to take a hard look at one or two books: Betty Friedan's *The Fountain of Age* and Gail Sheehy's *New Passages*.[20] The subtitle of the latter is especially important if one does, indeed, take Sheehy's advice seriously: "Mapping Your Life Across Time." If readers continue to ask while reading these books: "What does this imply for my learning?" they cannot miss the point that "the language of experience" is different for fifty-, sixty-, and ninety-year-olds than it was during their teens or thirties. As the title of my book suggests, I believe that the very word "retirement" (which includes the concept of being "tired") should be replaced by the word "re-FIRE-ment" (with the emphasis as indicated, being "fired" up to face each day with verve and the expectation of learning something new which will have practical or esthetic value). It helps to practice the mantra, "Give us this day, our daily surprise!"

Likewise "the body of experience" is different in both quantity and quality from what we possessed in earlier phases of our lives. This factor became more real to me when I followed Sheehy's lead and started some autobiographical writing by dividing my time map into decades and experience, somewhat as follows:

1–10 Babyhood and elementary school—basic learning habits traditional;

11–20 Teenage rebellions but how to be a good student—gluttony for knowledge—early industrial experience—college of hard knocks;

21–30 More industrial exposure, transfer of values to college and graduate school learning—skill in encountering traditional knowledge modes;

31–40 Finish Ph.D.—teaching in traditional mode—working closely with students; experiences in a Greek college screamed: *break out* of provincial ways—interest in larger arenas for learning;

41–50 Move to "big-time" university teaching; discomfort with traditional learning modes (big classes); break from church; reeducate myself about alternative ways of knowing; return to poetry;

51–60 Make radical shift to evolve person-centered learning at graduate levels—learn pros and cons of different

models of organization—difficulty of gaining acceptance of experimental education;

61–70 Dangers and opportunities of retiring into re-FIRE-
ment—excitement of being my own person quite free
of institutional straitjackets—ups and downs of being
an educational consultant and author;

71–80 Continuing seventh-decade insights into eighth decade.

This is, of course, sketchy and overgeneralized. It may seem like common sense, but what do we *do* with such knowledge? Some cultures, both nonliterate and literate, have honored and dignified experience and knowledge, giving that maturity and wisdom a place in the hierarchy of social organization. The very presence of elders has been important. But today, with the democratization of knowledge and its easy access, elders' wisdom does not seem to be so rare; they do not have a monopoly on wisdom; furthermore, there are more seniors, and the supply-demand formulas work differently. It is not unseemly to honor that African proverb: "When an old person dies, a library burns."

Aside: When a dear friend read the manuscript of this book and came upon this quotation, she wrote in the margin: "Choose one or more deceased relatives and explain what they gave you!" In the spirit of sharing my experience, I am responding to her challenge in the hope that you, the reader, will make your own list, perhaps in the context of your own decade-by-decade review of your life:

Father—a positive sense of endurance and unconditional love for many of his family and friends; love of story telling; strong work ethic; serving people;

Mother—positive sense of endurance and encouraging the quick and honest reaction; memory for fine details; strong work ethic;

Uncle Edward—negative—a sense of anger when I encounter bigotry and hatred for whole populations, a man who thought Hitler did the "right thing" in killing 6 million Jews;

Aunt Nellie—buoyant love of laughter, life, and food;

Aunt Eva—need for calm in a storm; strong work ethic;

Aunt Melissa—independent-mindedness, little fear of "what people will say"; appreciation and risk of living in Manhattan.

Senior learning is vitally important, not only for survival but also for the quality of life. One cannot afford to be unaware of the impact of legislation upon one's finances and future. One cannot be indifferent to crises in Medicare, Social Security, or Crime Watch. One cannot be insensitive to the implications of the age-old dictum to "seize the day." Learning is critical to survival no matter what one's race, gender, creed, or clan. It is important to avoid any structure *of any kind* that cuts us off from learning, whether it be a social group, a political party, or family bias that inhibits knowing. Only by knowing how "the facts of the world" impinge upon one's everyday existence can one live in a dignified manner.

Exercise No. 5: Your Own Passages

Read Sheehy's book closely; or if this seems difficult or impossible, find somebody who will read it to you.

Then place yourself in the appropriate generation which she defines in light of your birthdate.

On every page, ask these questions: Assuming the truth of her analysis, what difference does her viewpoint mean to me? What do I have to learn to live a better life today, tomorrow, and next week? And what do I mean by "better"? Do I need to seek counsel for better learning? Where? How? Wherein is my "mapping" of life unique for me?

The famous psychologist Carl Rogers wrote a book, *A Way of Being*, that contains a chapter that he titled "Growing Old: or Older and Growing?"[21] Ask yourself which state of being fits you better. (That choice may be used effectively in responding to some of the queries in the above paragraph.)

If you have never heard of the term "elderhostel," obtain their phone number and call them *today*. This organization deserves every accolade ever conceived to reward the humanizing of experience, with programs, both long and short, local and international, theoretical and experiential, practical and esoteric; pick and choose from this wonderful smorgasbord of learning nutrition. Finance the experience as you can. These supplements do not come in plastic containers, they are the living and vital tissues of being.

Three Cheers for Enthusiasm

It was said of Mark Twain that he had one enthusiasm per day and it was always "a storm." A *Miami Herald* staff writer, commenting upon Gary Sheffield, a major-league baseball player, remarked, "Desire doesn't simply drive him. It erupts in him." Two Bates College and Boston University professors, Angelo and Peter Bertocci, are frequently remembered by former students for their passionate teaching, their enthusiasm for their subject matter, and their ability to draw out their students. They inspired large numbers of us to enter the teaching profession. Also, their doors were always open if we needed help.

It is probably too much to expect everybody to sustain the energy for such creative eruptions; after all, temperaments differ person to person, but it doesn't seem too far-fetched to relate enthusiasm to learning. I see no barrier to adding *enthusiasm* to thanks for "daily bread." Since we tend to become that which we think (as well as what we eat), simply uttering a morning wish, "Give us this day, our daily enthusiasm," might go far to produce the fact. But why be enthusiastic in the first place?

Aside: My dear friend, mentioned above, also challenged me to cite some of my own "creative eruptions." Not an easy thing to do if they come fairly regularly, but I told her that I would try:

- In November 1938, during the infamous recession that necessitated a four-day week and while listening to an uncle and a friend discuss what they would do "if they had $1,000," I blurted out, "I'd go to college!" That chance outburst, on a "laid-off day" when I would have otherwise been doing my factory job, led me to college.

- In 1956, when searching for a title for the history of my hometown, Saco, Maine, I was scanning book titles in the Bates College library and happened to spy *Wind, Sand and Stars,* which I translated in split seconds into

Sands, Spindles and Steeples, three symbols characterizing the town from 1630 to 1950. It's a book title people seem to remember long after they've forgotten details of the town's history.

- In the early 1990s, when participating in an effort to enable a section of the Maine coast to secede from the city of Biddeford and learning that citizens in more than a dozen other sections felt similarly, I put all the factors together and very rapidly wrote an article called "Coastalvania," recommending (perhaps whimsically) that they get together and form a political unit, connect it with the Internet, and probably experience more civic freedom and responsibility than currently enjoyed.

- As an inveterate wordmonger, most of my poems and essays grow out of the constant conversations in my head regarding alternative viewpoints and modes of expressing viewpoints. Sooner or later one is bound to pop out, be captured by my enthusiasm, and find the light of day. Perhaps it's something like that analogy that is sometimes used regarding animal intelligence and probability: put enough chimpanzees at typewriters in a gymnasium for a long enough time, and one of them may come up with a line from Shakespeare!

In an essay written more than a half century ago, social commentator H. Addington Bruce advocated the "Importance of Being Interested."[22] He knew enough psychology to realize that we learn best when we focus best and with intensity. But "interest" can sketch many faces. We've all seen enough children's faces light up when they became excited or friends wax enthusiastic in telling a story, so we can identify with their emotions. We are certainly well aware that boredom results from lack of relating. As kids we're bored if we have "nothing to do." In school we're bored if nothing is happening that grabs our attention. At work as adults, we wither on the vine if we're not challenged or work is slack (even if the pay is good). At home we sometimes become "couch potatoes" by watching steady streams of television that numb the mind. Sometimes it's difficult to differentiate one program from another or a news item from a commercial if the story of a shooting immediately follows one about a Nobel Prize! Ironically enough, we may know more about what bores us than what excites us. Hence, perhaps it's time for another inventory.

Exercise No. 6: Your Enthusiasm Quotient

Make a list of activities or topics that bore you.

> Make a list of activities or topics that excite you, positively or negatively, it matters not. Do you have "creative eruptions"? When? Do you find a pattern? Can you induce them if challenged to do so?

> When were you last so enthusiastic about an event, happening, or topic that you could hardly eat or sleep? Why? Short-term learning from it? Long-range learning?

> Can you work out a schedule or program whereby boring events or topics can be minimized in your daily life? maximized? Could you invent a unique personal system wherein you might estimate how newly discovered topics,

interests, and enthusiasms affect your attitudes? Your health in general? Your zest for life?

Can you find role models, such as Mark Twain, or a professional athlete, a musician, a painter, or other prominent person whose life, work, and promise have suggested ways to enhance your enthusiasms? How? Meaning?

Is this the kind of topic which you can discuss openly with your family so that you might obtain some reinforcement for New Ventures in Enthusiasm?

Could you develop an EQ (Enthusiasm Quotient) to guide you?

New Learning Styles for Traditional Institutions

There's an old saying in higher-education circles that "it's easier to move a cemetery than a faculty." Hence, changes in curriculum move like glaciers, especially weeding out defunct courses from college catalogues. But some of the major changes that have occurred since World War II have highlighted shifts in learning modes:

- The GI Bill provided the means for military veterans to advance to college and they came with experience that challenged their peers, faculty, and institutions. The presence of ex-GIs added ferment to the classrooms in particular and campus life in general. No faculty could afford to make unsubstantiated generalizations or peddle false data and in some cases use old, outmoded lecture notes. Veterans were highly focused, not only to obtain degrees but also to learn. They challenged both faculty and institutions to be honest about *what* and *how* they knew, and also no fooling around when it came to students' rights.

- The Student Dissent Movement in the late 1960s and early 1970s challenged institutions around the issue of "relevance" of curriculum, the fairness of governance, and the utilization of graduate students as teacher assistants. At one point in the early 1970s, more than four hundred institutions of higher education were shut down. Violence frequently broke out. Shootings at Kent State and Jackson State had a profound impact upon student life and learning, and also alerted the country to some of the Achilles' heels of academia.

- Demographic pressures on colleges and universities, wherein the number of eligible eighteen-year-olds leveled off or declined, literally forced the institutions (especially those that had expanded rapidly after WWII) to seek students, with tuition, elsewhere. Hence the rapid expansion of adult and/or "continuing education." It is my considered opinion that, despite word music to the contrary, most such expansions were based upon economics rather than belief in or understanding of adult learning. Grand old laborers in the adult-learning vineyards, persons such as Malcolm Knowles, a professor and researcher in adult education who had for decades observed in writing and from the lecture platform that adults learn differently than youth, came into their own. More frequently than not, however, such "continuing" programs were perceived by "regular faculty" as "second class." Amazingly enough, some institutions such as the University of Miami creamed off the net income (profit) with practically none of that yearly profit retained by the entrepreneurial College of Continuing Education; thus creating a *dis*-incentive. Yet, let it be said on behalf of those who continued to invent programs relevant to the greater Miami community (capital of the "Floribian" or Florida-Caribbean), the *dis*-incentive did not deter their efforts.

- Immigration and expansion of community/junior college is another topic relevant to changed learning styles and their challenge to traditional institutions. When, for instance, a Los Angeles or Miami Beach elementary-school classroom has as many as twenty to forty students whose native language is not English, the teacher must call upon every device in the arsenal of pedagogy to encourage learning as well as coping! In addition, mainstreaming laws in most states as well as handicapped-access laws at the federal level exert similar pressures, whether the unique students are fresh "off the boat," are paraplegic, or nonsighted. At the higher-education level, local institutions such as Miami-Dade Community College (MDCC) have met the specific needs of immigrants, fresh from the Caribbean, offering programs which address linguistic needs, business and technology skills, and the foundation for advancing to four-year schools and on into the professions of medicine, law, and scientific research.

- Unique institutions such as Elderhostel (both national and international); adult programs such as "Great Decisions" and "Great Books" as well as various professional associations attached to both community and university facilities are providing a wide variety of opportunities wherein seniors can participate in seminars, artistic performances (accompanied by discussions), and films and are providing a variety of and more widely available learning options than the country has ever known. In Naples, Florida, for instance, Dr. Calvin Leonard has created an extraordinarily mature and imaginative Lifelong Learning program so rich in opportunity to keep up with the arts and social issues that it is difficult to imagine any adult who could afford *not* to participate if she really wanted to adapt her learning style to the learning and programs offered.

- The professions, too, occupy a living presence on the "adult education" stage in the name of "keeping up" standards and professional competence and advancement. In Connecticut, for instance, teachers must earn a quota of Certified Educational Units (CEUs) in order to retain their licenses. In the healthcare professions similar requirements are established to keep practitioners "up to snuff" with the latest in knowledge of drugs, surgical procedures, and technological advances. Since most "adult education" is decentralized, it is left pretty much to the professions via the professional associations to determine standards and the efficacy of advanced training. Members are expected to subscribe to journals as a means of maintaining current knowledge and skills. It is also expected that persons serving in these several professions, from education to medicine to law, will police themselves via ethics committees, licensing processes, and legal appeals in violations cases. Critics of the several professions sometimes argue that this is similar to sending out the fox to guard the chicken coop, and there is usually plenty of data to support such contentions. But unless we wish to develop a police state, there are bound to be people and practices that fall through the grids. It is to be hoped that these are the exception rather than the rule and that some checks and balances do help create what we sometimes call "a free society."

• Corporate learning today certainly goes far beyond traditional modalities of a decade or two ago. Teleconferencing, even when it's didactic, reflects changing technological opportunities for employees. Corporations the world over recognize changing technologies, changing marketplaces, changing human needs—in fact, change is probably the only constant that exists in the marketplace. New and relevant learning is both qualitatively and quantitatively related to survival. And in a global village where "the survival of the fittest" becomes the ultimate test in the vogue of Social Darwinism, learning about the survival syndrome may be as valuable for the world citizen as learning about the potentials and implications of satellite information. Surely, as George Soros, the world-renown investor and philanthropist, argues in "The Capitalist Threat,"[23] in view of the laissez-faire era which has succeeded in dominating the world economy with the collapse of fascism and communism, world citizens must find new learning modes and rhythms to adjust to the dangers and opportunities of the systems in which they are involved. There seems to be much wisdom in the Chinese pictogram where one figure depicts both danger and opportunity:

As suggested above, the democratization of the Internet will continue to put extraordinary pressure on traditional institutions. As one of my colleagues, Paul Haber, who is deeply immersed in and a student of this phenomenon, indicated in a recent e-mail communication:

A lot of universities are getting on line now with so-called independent study programs. The current and oft-used hot acronym is GIS for "guided independent studies." Most of these universities are only masquerading as GIS programs. Brigham Young [BY] is an excellent example. Their only GIS faculty are traditional educators who teach regular classes at BY who have via computer education become "faculty" to on-line learners. Courses are as structured and sterile as the classroom courses that they teach with little or more often no room for creativity or learner pursuit of interests within the area of study they are taking . . . other institutions which offer independent-study programs at this point in time, are not interested in hiring additional faculty with backgrounds in GIS. Their courses are basically the same courses a learner would get in a classroom except they're being done via e-mail and the Net. I've been calling it traditional courses without classrooms, or TCWC.

The problem is that the traditional faculties for most of these courses don't believe that learning is possible if it's not under their strict physical supervision and because they don't trust learners (most of whom are adults who have gone back to school and make the best learners); they often require even more from distance learners taking a course, than they do from learners taking the same course in a classroom. . . . Many learners understand the rationale behind this and are damned angry about it . . . [in fact] in conversations refer to themselves as grown adults with a lot of life experience who are being treated as children by educational institutions and express an awareness that they aren't getting what they need from the institutions and a knowledge that they do have options.[24]

Dr. Haber goes on to note that there are options to these "cloaked traditional programs," hence they are skeptical of "duplicitous advertising campaigns . . . that present themselves as GIS but are really traditional and are on line." And therein Paul Haber has put his finger on the major pulse of the issue; namely, lack of trust and misrepresentation. The Internet does, indeed, offer one of the most unique opportunities in the history of learning. Learning is no longer just open to the privileged only, whether church; dominant political, economic, or social groups; professional groups; or other traditional elites. But institutions who have been standing for both traditional values and evolving opportunities cannot live with those contradictions much longer. And not all Internet data are necessarily reliable.

If we don't learn anything from life, regardless of our unique learning style, we learn that things are rarely as they seem. Hence it is my belief that each of us can develop literacy in dealing with irony and paradox, to appreciate the complexity of situations; and also in doing it, learn that laughter "may be our last best cope." Furthermore, I suggest various forms of expression in which you may present your view to the world in unique ways.

Notes

1. *Time* 149, no. 6 (February 3, 1997).

2. Marilyn Ferguson, *The Aquarian Conspiracy* (Los Angeles: J. P. Tarcher, 1980), pp. 289–291; Maria Montessori, *Spontaneous Activity in Education* (New York: Schocken Books, 1965).

3. Shakespeare, *Hamlet* 1.2.

4. Neil Postman and Charles Weingartner, *Teaching as a Subversive Activity* (New York: Delacorte Press, 1969).

5. Barbara Kingsolver, *The Poisonwood Bible* (New York: Harper Flamingo, 1998).

6. A term used by Professor Troy Organ both in a faculty lecture at Ohio University and in private conversation when we were colleagues in Athens, Ohio.

7. Roy Fairfield, "Freedom Is Frightening," *Free Inquiry* 1, no. 1 (1980): 30–31.

8. *Miami Herald*, February 7, 1997.

9. Roy P. Fairfield, *Person-Centered Graduate Education* (Amherst, N.Y.: Prometheus Books, 1977).

10. Kent State University, *Distributed Learning Policy Recommendations* (Kent, Ohio: December 1996).

11. Alfred North Whitehead, *Science and the Modern World* (New York: Pelican Mentor Edition, 1948), p. 52.

12. From "The Tables Turned."

13. See any of the several books by Michael Q. Patton.

14. Traditional sociologist who resigned in a huff as adjunct professor when he encountered my wisecrack/critique of "the religion of objectivity"; I've always wished he might have stuck around to engage me directly. Perhaps we both could have learned from the encounter.

15. Bertrand Russell, *New York Times Magazine* (December 16, 1951).

16. Roy P. Fairfield, "The Dignity of Hands," *Humanist* 32, no. 3 (1972): 36–37.

17. Roy P. Fairfield, "To Saw a Board," *Humanist* 35, no. 1 (1975): 37–39.

18. Chris Cernich, "The Romance of Old Tools," *Newsweek* (September 18, 1995): 16.

19. Roy P. Fairfield, *Humanizing the Workplace* (Amherst, N.Y.: Prometheus Books, 1974).

20. Betty Friedan, *The Fountain of Age* (New York: Simon & Schuster, 1993); Gail Sheehey, *New Passages* (New York: Random House, 1995).

21. Carl Rogers, *A Way of Being* (Boston: Houghton & Mifflin, 1980), pp. 70–95.

22. H. Addington Bruce, "Importance of Being Interested," in *The New College Omnibus*, ed. Arthur Fullington (New York: Harcourt, Brace, 1938), pp. 95–101.

23. George Soros, "The Capitalist Threat," *Atlantic* 281, no. 2 (1997): 45–58.

24. Permission to reprint granted by telephone, March 2, 2001.

CHAPTER 4

Paradox, Irony, and Freedom (to Laugh)

Paucity and Audacity

Few would argue that paucity of "this, that, and the other" tends to dominate human life—or at least even in a world of plenty, there seems to be a constant scarcity of something that everybody wants. If it's not food, it can be love; if it's not peace, it can be noise, and so on. And the psychology of surfeit is amply symbolized in Dante's *Inferno* where the so-called sins of greed, lust, and other fleshly "evils" live on in characters doomed to repeat them endlessly through all eternity—a frightening prospect which supposedly scared Christians to "shape up," be repentant, or spend forever in Hell! Yet, it is my strongest conviction that perceiving events in terms of Paradox and Irony both permits and encourages the freedom to laugh—at self, society, ridiculous contradictions, absurdities, and so on. Of course, believing this as I do means that I live much of my life bathing in Paradox, Irony, and Humor. Try collecting headlines such as: "To Achieve Success, Try Failure," an article in which the author says, "All of my successes are the products of my failures. Rejection did not teach me what to do so much as force me to go beyond what I had done, to try a new way."[1] Also, I like the oft-quoted observation by Paul

Gauguin, the French painter, "I shut my eyes in order to see." Sensitivity to such paradoxes inevitably leads to new learning, new thinking, and new action.

In my book *Person-Centered Graduate Education*, I encounter paradoxes every time I turn around; for instance, why seek a Ph.D. if one simply wants to learn? And why should a group of person-centered learners ask me to *lecture to* them? But as I describe that occasion in chapter 11, I decided to talk about "Some Things I've Learned," listing them in no particular order but in dramatic enough fashion to enlist their attention:

1. One of the most difficult things to develop is the courage to *let be*.[2]
2. I have no desire to be a member of any college or university department.
3. The closer one is to the center of power, the less one has.
4. Learning is a function of size; also the spoken word is a bummer.
5. Idealism is a bummer; seeking perfection can easily kill you.
6. To be of use, you must take abuse.
7. Every student's major is identity-searching—nobody has a corner on the market of being oppressed.
8. Relevance *is* relevant.
9. The higher one's profile, the less likely he'll get things done.
10. The central task of the learning process is to structure conditions leading to self-discovery of paradox, humor, and irony.

It would be redundant to repeat more of that chapter where I spin out more notions of the same sort. Strange thing, however,

I've not modified these viewpoints very much in three decades although today I'd probably find a synonym for "bummer" and add to no. 6: "if one is engaged in social situations" (teaching, politics, marketing, etc.).

One of the many problems resulting from the normal use of Western linear logic as the basis for action or analysis is the fact that this sometimes obscures the need for alternative perspectives. It's important to remind ourselves occasionally of some of these alternatives. For instance, Parker Palmer, in his *Courage to Teach*, reminds us that, "The opposite of a true statement is a false statement, but the opposite of a profound truth can be another profound truth." So what is "truth" but "a paradoxical joining of apparent opposites" which "we must learn to embrace these efforts as one."[3]

Sometimes wisecracks sharpen the nature of paradox; for instance:

- If at first you don't succeed, skydiving is not for you.

- If you are given an open-book exam, you will forget where your book is.

- The trouble with doing something right the first time is that nobody appreciates how difficult it was.[4]

Then, too, here's another provocative headline, from an essay by journalist Pico Iyer, "The Eloquent Sounds of Silence."[5] As implied above, once sensitive to paradox, such headlines jump off the page at you! Also, it sets the creative juices flowing, as can be seen by the following.

Fairfield's Laws

Everybody is certainly entitled and to be encouraged to create at least one "law" in his own name during a lifetime. As one looks about and becomes more familiar with idiosyncrasies, idiocies, and eidetic images (deep imprints at first observation), it is next to impossible to avoid seeing patterns, whether in vulgarities or continuities, that could be projected into "law." For instance, if one returns to the dawn of Greek consciousness and/or reflection about the nature of the world, one finds Thales claiming that "all is water" whereas Heraclitis says that "all is fire since the only thing constant is change." Yet, not to be outdone, the French coined a phrase some centuries later, "Plus ça change, plus c'est la même chose," i.e., the more things change the more they're the same. So we encounter decalogue after decalogue which seem to argue for rules in human behavior. . . . These may be helpful or hurtful references, but the rules enable one to know where he stands vis-à-vis the law. For instance, Moses declared that God wanted us to love Him with all our might (rather a circular piece of logic, or at least filled with Cosmic Ego); whereas the British philosopher Bertrand Russell advised us "not to respect the authority of others, for there are always contrary authorities to be found." Ironically, one assumes that one must be skeptical even of Russell's law.

My own entrance into translating observation into law-making evolved from watching colleges and universities leap from relatively humane scales of size into huge, bureaucratic complexes that tended to dehumanize the entire academic world. In fact, the more they grew, the more rapidly they became obsolete. Hence, I compiled my First Law:

THE MORE THAT CAMPUS SPACES OPEN,
THE FASTER THEY FILL UP AND BECOME OBSOLETE.

Something like the major-league pitcher Satchel Paige observing, "The faster I run, the behinder I get"—a twist from common-sense logic to paradox and humor.

The same observation is easily applicable to highways.

THE BIGGER THEY GET, THE QUICKER THEIR OBSOLESCENCE.

Strange, too, since one would think that highway planners could quickly see this and cease expansion. Or perhaps they know it already, but scramble for more contracts to maintain their economic bases of operation.

Surely, there must be laws growing out of the 1990s phenomenon of downsizing. If one can generalize beyond the "situational" or corporate "ethics" as reflected in Scott Adams's hot comic strip, "Dilbert," most readers will find ironies and paradoxes in current corporate culture. But even without in-depth analysis of Adams's critique of the contemporary corporate world, it's fairly easy to derive other laws which contain the seeds of irony and/or paradox:

THE FULLER EMPLOYMENT IS, THE GREATER PROBABILITY OF
INFLATION AND HENCE RECESSION/DEPRESSION.

THE MORE ONE WORRIES ABOUT BEING UNEMPLOYED, THE GREATER
THE PROBABILITY OF BEHAVIOR LEADING TO BEING FIRED.

THE MORE PRESSURE ON THE POCKETBOOK AND DEMAND
(OR UNION ACTIVITY) TO IMPROVE WAGES/SALARIES,
THE GREATER PROBABILITY OF BEING DOWNSIZED.

THE MORE STRENUOUS THE SEARCH FOR CERTAINTY,
THE MORE CERTAIN THE UNCERTAINTY.

UNPOPULAR CAUSES BECOME POPULAR WHEN ATTACKED.

THYME AND SAGE (OR DILL) WAIT FOR NO WOMAN.

Sadly enough, the application of such laws is not only micro-important but also macro. It ill behooves sensitive persons *not* to develop such laws for themselves to keep their laughing muscles active!

> Aside: One's internal dialogue might run: "So I pushed too hard, my labor union lost, and we all got fired!" (shades of Reagan's firing the airport controllers, also "chicken" that airline pilots "play" games with their airlines periodically). How foolish I was to think that our history encourages us to be individualistic when, indeed, we are interdependent and rely upon so many forces beyond our control. Not only "foolish" but laughably paradoxical! To wit: Reagan fired the air controllers, yet had an airport named for him (Washington National!).

If the American educational system flunks any topic, endeavor, or process with distinction, it's that which I call "irony and paradox literacy." We have been wrapped up in the logic of consistency for so long that we do poorly in analyzing situations requiring new viewpoints that are contradictory, no matter the criteria we use in looking at the data. For instance, an easy verbal illustration: "I'll kill you if you're not for peace."

A social illustration: Spending more money for new prisons than schools.

We can find such an illustration, too, in a Moscow joke:

> The optimist sighs, "At least things can't get worse."
> His sister optimist observes, "Sure they can."[6]

1 1 3

My personal bias: most persons are able to look at daily events and articulate such ironies and/or paradoxes. Hence:

Exercise No. 7: Your Paradox Quotient (PQ)

Reflect upon major events in your own life during the past few weeks, months, and years and record some of those ironies and/or paradoxes which you've encountered.

Taking it a step further: scan the newspapers and/or television programs wherein ironies and/or paradoxes are so numerous.

Distance yourself from such analyses and/or experiences to see if you can laugh at the absurdities; the ridiculous, comic aspects of the "human comedy." Take a hard look at stand-up comics' programs such as Mark Russell's to see how many of them are founded upon such ironies and paradoxes; or pick up writings by Mark Twain, H. L. Mencken, or James Thurber to enjoy the fully mature development of themes on this topic. Ambrose Bierce's *Devil's Dictionary* might also provide insights.

Also, think through an observation that Stephen Leacock, the Canadian humorist, made when he defined a "college education" as "what you have left over after you've forgotten all that you ever learned!"

Invent your own paradoxes for a fuller appreciation of their significance; nor should you hesitate to laugh at them!

Fables

Another way to enjoy/appreciate this process is to write fables. Writing fables is a healthy way to blow off steam about issues that are too painful to contemplate, too complex to simplify, too funny to take seriously, or compensate for love or money.

As I say in the "Foreview" of my book, *Seaside Fables and Other Incites,*

> The fable as a form of human expression has existed for at least twenty-five centuries of Western literature. Aesop, writing in Greece around the sixth century B.C. is the classical author best known to Americans; yet, Chaucer, Jean de La Fontaine, Gotthold Lessing, John Gay, all regaled their times with charming tales that serve as commentary and/or entertainment. In our own time George Orwell's *Animal Farm*, a book-length critique of both communism and fascism, is fabulous!
>
> No matter the fablist's style or focus, most fables are commentaries on human folly. While both the story and moral of the story may seem simple (even simpleminded), fables frequently, indeed, carry a heavy bite. They can also be a kind of shield for those wishing to use them, a shield to protect the user against repression or even death. After all, the fablist can argue, the characters are animals, hence may safely say, "Who, me? I didn't say that, it was the lion, the hare, or the fox who said that, surely not me!" In medieval times Reynard the Fox was an epic that introduced an entire cast of animals who were adapted to a variety of situations. During the German occupation of France, during World War II, for instance, fables served as effective covers against German intimidation. They have been used in American political campaigns when one candidate wished to satirize another.[7]

This is to encourage everybody to experiment with the form. Let me suggest an approach to such creations via the anatomy of the first fable in my book.

As a founder of the Union Graduate School, now the Union Institute, I was hard pressed after the first two years of the program's existence (1970–72) to respond to a fairly large number of persons who wanted to claim some of the "glory" for its success. In many ways each had contributed to the concept and its execution, both before and after our first learners matriculated. In some respects, too, most of the would-be "founders" were aware that we were risking our very existence in *seeming* to compete with the modes of doctoral education that had existed for decades. But I also knew that those of us "in the trenches" were evolving a process that had no clear starting point. We were innovating, even improvising, each step of the way. Under this kind of pressure (which always seems to put new energies into my angles of vision), it suddenly occurred to me:

EVERY ILLEGITIMATE CREATURE WHO BECOMES
FAMOUS HAS MANY FOUNDING FATHERS.

Hence, the moral for a fable was born. Working backward from that moral, I wrote the fable fairly quickly, only changing a word or two after sharing it with the Union Graduate School world, which included those claiming to be founders. Here is the fable:

Two flocks of wild geese, one solid black and the other pure white, clashed in a checkerboard promontory landscape. Feathers flew in clouds, and the whirring of wings woke people for miles around on that eerie dawn. As they disentangled, the flocks flew in opposite directions, all birds a dull gray except for one lonely creature who emerged with clearly marked black and white stripes, a goose so unique he was pursued over vast territories, captured, and carried to a zoo where he became world famous. Ornithologists from many nations came to see him, likewise farmers, teachers and their students, and members of every profession . . . all claiming him as their own.

Hence, the Moral: Every illegitimate creature who becomes famous has many founding fathers.

At about the same time my own input, both conceptually and operationally, was so demanding that I began calling myself "the founding mother"! Only a few militant feminists protested my marriage to whim and human folly![8] I venture to observe that there are few persons reading this who haven't been involved in a situation where a well-honed fable might have extricated them from an awkward position and at the very least been psychologically satisfying! Likewise the use of:

Do-It-Yourself Kits 2

Not long after retiring into what I prefer to call re-FIRE-ment, I began to compose and share a series of do-it-yourself kits. Similar to the Write-in-the-Dark Kit (see chapter 2), they included a large range of human activities, from amateur acupuncture to flatulation to writing haiku. I shared them widely, and received many suggestions for revising them and/or writing about other topics. Also, I received a few angry reactions to the more scatological missives! While I wrote most of them in a ten-year period, I continue to write them whenever my whimsy strikes me.

They are fairly easy to write and may pertain to any human activity and/or function. Much as David Letterman makes ten-point lists, intended to induce laughter, they need not necessarily include a logically sequential group of points as one might expect if assembling a toy auto kit or piece of furniture. Such kits may include whimsy; off-beat observations or instructions; juxtaposed opposites; *anything* that's fun, absurd, playful, humorous, satirical, hysterical, and so on. Above all, they must be *fun* to write and share. You'll also find that it probably makes no difference if you stand the kits on their head, as I have done in my Do-It-Yourself Re-FIRE-ment Kit (see epilogue).

A similar one which I once enjoyed sharing with my college classes and community lectures when things got dull, perhaps dealing with medieval food or contemporary culinary art; it seemed to matter not because reading it never failed to evoke laughter and provocative discussions.

How to Make a Cake [9]

Buy the package.

Consult Iva Haddit's *Cooking for Male Dummies* for instructions on how to open package.

Dump ingredients into mixing bowl.

Answer phone. Wrong number!

Reread instructions. Turn on TV for baseball game.

Answer doorbell. Mormon missionaries; accept literature.

Add water (with a dash of gin; sip gin).

Mix ingredients. Answer phone! "NO, NO! I don't want any!"

Take out 9" × 12" pan, butter inside.

Spouse returns from grocery shopping; needs help emptying car.

Untie apron, make five trips to carry all groceries to kitchen.

Add grumble to mixture.

Pour batter into pan just as favorite major-league batter steps to plate on TV.

Reset oven from 675 degrees to prescribed 350.

Add a deep breath to the atmosphere for having averted catastrophe; Havitt's book for *Male Dummies* didn't warn me.

Watch game; fold and pack both brown and plastic bags from grocery spree; peek at batter peaking in pan; answer doorbell; registered letter needs signature; spouse screams, "Cake's overflowing-g-g!"

Open oven as batter reaches the plate and hits the first pitch for a triple; I mean cake batter runs over side of pan and reaches the red-hot unit in oven and bursts into flame. I, too, boil over when next batter strikes out. No cake tonight.

Lie down for a nap.

Incidently, this book encourages creative ways of reacting to the world; it doesn't always need to be explained or "make sense."

Exercise No. 8: More Tooling Up

Choose a topic involving construction of an object or repairing a household appliance; then employing your wildest imagination, develop a kit guaranteed to make you and your family laugh for all of its absurdity. For instance, you might start a chili-making kit, for use on hot nights:

Go to ten neighbors and borrow every size frying pan you can find.

or start a kit for repairing a bicycle chain:

Dismantle a bicycle into every last piece, down to the last spoke of both wheels.

Using absurdity and/or the ridiculous as your instruments of choice, defy logic, defy gravity, defy common sense; use imagination; *think* wildly. After all, you don't have to share with anybody if you believe it yourself!

Potpourri of Decalogues

I have made previous reference to Bertrand Russell's "A New Decalogue" (see chapter 2).[10] While it's worth reading as a whole, this is to cite only a couple more commandments beyond those mentioned above. One may easily see how his viewpoints contrast with the historic biblical dicta.

No. 1. Do not feel absolutely certain of anything.

No. 3. Never try to discourage thinking, for you are sure to succeed.

No. 6. Do not use power to suppress opinions you think pernicious, for if you do the opinions will suppress you.

Russell was a world-class logician and well aware of the history of thought. He used these two skills, as well as brilliant insight into irony and paradox, when compiling his Decalogue. One need not be such a master, simply a careful observer of the human scene, as in writing fables and do-it-yourself kits, to write decalogues. I will include both the serious and the absurd.

I wrote the following after a decade or so of trying to live humanistically. The test here relates to the discovery of irony and paradox.

1. Honor thine own and thy neighbor's spaces.
2. Develop the courage to *let* be. (See Tillich's *Courage to Be.*)

3. Give us this day, our daily enthusiasm. (See chapter 3.)

4. Feel comfortable in the school of life with identity-searching as your major field of study.

5. Take seriously thine own joy in humor, irony, and paradox.

6. To be of use in human service, you must take abuse. (Repeat nightly!)

7. Treat your neighbor as both horizon and parameter.

8. Seek self-actualization.

9. Listen closely to your pains of sorrow, fear, and anxiety, but eschew guilt with a passion. (It's paralytic!)

10. Substitute any of your own human rules for any/all of the above.

Those observations evolved from a ten-year period when I served on more than five-hundred doctoral committees, a period of my life which I've stated in hyperbolic terms: "I regret I had only forty years to give to the Union Graduate School during the Decade of the Seventies." I probably learned more about human psychology in that time than I'd have learned in fifty courses in psychology, sociology, and philosophy. Yet, I called this summary "A Humanistic Decalogue."

But I've conceived many others of a more facetious nature. Here are a sampling of commandments from several others:

Decalogue for Survival of Teachers in the Public School

1. Thou shalt wear the standard school costume, "all uv drab."
3. Thou shalt keep silence in thy classroom, lest learning seem joyful.

4. Thou shalt not joke with the principal . . . or about principles, even with unprincipled principals!
8. Thou shalt worship the textbook with all thy heart, with all thy "mind," and with all thy pocketbook.

Decalogue for College Faculty

1. Thou shalt work hard at scholarly pursuits, but be no more diligent (or prolific) than thy chairperson or dean.
4. Thou must keep at least one paragraph, book, or monograph, musical score, or mathematical theorem ahead of your students; but, be not dismayed if the brighter ones read, compose, and rush ahead to the finish line and are standing there waiting to greet you when you arrive!
5. During accreditation visits, thou shalt wear a neck brace to keep your head nodding affirmatives; dissent is unpopular. Take Lockjaw Lessons, too, so you can in good conscience be silent. Wear *not* a canary yellow sweater, scarlet dress, or other distinguishable clothing. If you stand *out*, you'll be unable to stand *back* when the visiting firemen and women project their criticisms at you, lest you become a symbol of what they disapprove of.
10. In preparation for commencement exercises and other forced marches, thou shalt refrain from eating bananas which will come up too easily if the rhetoric makes you gag.
11. [SURPRISE! Most decalogues have only ten points.] Thou shalt learn to laugh at every idiocy from official-dumb and translate it into irony and paradox. Also practice the exercise of imagining yourself in your academic casket, complete with school-colored cap, gown, hood, and smile, smirk, or guffaw . . . with teeth showing.[11]

Surely we've all attended enough meetings where *Robert's Rules of Order* were in force so literally and nauseatingly that we've been compelled to run to the public john for relief. The chair is frequently such a control freak that it's no wonder that a prominent Maine political observer responded as he did to a question from a distinguished sociologist about a town meeting: The question: "What's the function of the moderator?" The cryptic response: "To keep the bastards down!" With all this in mind as well as attending several dehumanizing humanist meetings, I devised what I called "Robots Rules of Order" for the Union Graduate School. Here are commandments for the more recent faculty, prone to wink at the eroded vision:

1. Always remember that the Union is ultimately a top-down organization, hence do not feel denigrated by being treated as a puppet or "boy/girl." You've "asked for it" many times by refusing to protest the obvious destruction of academic due process.
2. You must specialize in illusion construction. (See chapter 8.)
3. Begin each day with a mantra that carries the essential message: *Dissent is bad . . . Dissent is bad . . . Dissent is bad!* And its counterpart: *Obedience is good! . . . Obedience is good!*
5. Even if you know that "mastery of an academic field" is impossible today, or even irrelevant, don't admit it—even in your subconscious "mind"! Anti-illusionists will never know the difference!
7. No matter how convinced you may be that "standards of excellence" are phony or that "being professional" is to espouse mediocrity, learn not to admit it!
8. Remember Huxley's dictum in *Brave New World* that 2,032 repetitions equal one truth.

9. Repeat mantralike, "Yes sir, yes sir, yes sir," ad infinitum. It will convince you of your role as robot. Also, you will be better prepared to answer your students/learners without committing yourself. If necessary, go to the woods or seashore to practice your mantra and get used to hearing your own voice and name. Also bureau-*crazy* responses.
10. Invent a commandment that grows out of your experience. (A warm-up for Exercise No. 9 below.)

Those familiar with the genuine *Robert's Rules* will have no difficulty translating some of these concepts into another decalogue, especially for use in small groups or where the course Awareness 101–102 is profoundly needed.

Finally, to a decalogue that was most fun to write. As I began training West Cameroon Peace Corps volunteers in 1962, one of my academic colleagues, Otto Krash (a "semi-demi, quasi-pseudo mentor" [his words!], known to his students as Dr. Train Wreck), challenged me to write a decalogue. I invited him to contribute. We brainstormed for an entire evening and had such a hilarious experience our diaphragms were sore for a week. Among the commandments:

2. Thou shalt not conceive of marrying an indigene without consulting the West Cameroon Peace Corps rep, the U.S. ambassador, the Peace Corps director, Secretary of State Rusk, your mother, President Kennedy —and incidentally, the indigene's father!
4. Thou shalt not covet the ambassadorship—unless you can afford it.
5. Do not consider yourself a shining light, even in Darkest Africa.

8. Thou shalt not include in your overseas baggage:
   yoyos, hula hoops, raccoon coats, Frisbees, bubblegum
   baseball cards, tattoo guns, gallon cans of fingernail polish,
   the *Congressional Record*, gift subscriptions to *Mad*; nor
   charge the U.S. government for hometown telephone direc-
   tories, electric blankets, blenders and dishwashers, sports
   cars, suburban value structures, political party platforms,
   and social prejudices.
9. Thou shalt not spin myths about the United States, such
   as:
   America is invincible, George Washington liked cherries,
   Edgar Allen Poe belonged to AA, GOP stands for gawd-
   orful politics.

We added a "Bonus Commandment," namely, Thou shalt not lose
thy sense of humor.

Exercise No. 9: Your Personal Commandments

1. Write your own decalogue to gain appreciation of the
   process and its life value for you. Can you obey it?
2. If at first you don't succeed, on your own terms, try doing
   one as a spoof on yourself; then, try again.

In short, the decalogue is another tool for expounding upon
the fool in each of us. It may be filled with irony, paradox, creative cynicism, far-fetched ideas, absurdity, hilarity, and non-
sense. As with most writing, it will enable you to clarify and
purify your own understanding of self and your relationship to
other persons and organizations with which you are associated.
It's an opportunity to say what you think about your own

behavior; after all, you need not *necessarily* share your decalogues with anybody, much as you might like to command respect from everybody!

Jester Letters

Many years ago, on a day when my high-school daughter and I were kidding around a lot, out of a clear blue sky she said, "Daddy, you ought to be Jester at the White House!" I had proposed creating that position many times, even in my classes, but I'd never considered inventing or lobbying for the job myself. But her comment touched off a series of thoughts and actions. I literally did turn down a Washington job offer, with the wisecrack, "There's only one job in D.C. that I would take, Jester at the White House." To paraphrase the notion that war is too important to be left to the generals, it seemed fairly obvious that governing is too serious to be left to the politicians. But other than joking about it, I did nothing to move in that direction until Ronald Reagan became president of the United States the same month that I retired into re-FIRE-ment and began looking for projects to accompany ten other things I'd planned to do. So I conceived the idea of writing a series of Jester Letters to the White House (i.e., to Reagan and members of his administration). I was under no delusion that many if any messages would get through, but I thought it might be fun to try. After all, as citizens we are encouraged to write to our representatives. Why not start at the top?

During Reagan's first year in office, I wrote 149 letters to the White House. Most of them, of course, landed on desert soil. Twenty percent of the answers were no doubt "form letters" and some seemed to divert my name to the list of potential donors to the Republican Party. Yet a few were interesting and worth sharing:

To Michael Deaver, Deputy Chief of Staff, I congratulated him and his staff for

> *Not* waking the president . . . following the U.S.–Libyan encounter in air space over the Mediterranean. When/if an atomic holocaust arrives, I think that yesterday's decision . . . provides a good model . . . a humane one since he might never know what hit him. [I went on to] recommend that you begin to collect old Marx Brothers, Laurel and Hardy, W. C. Fields, etc. films that could be used much as Norman Cousins used them as described in his *Anatomy of an Illness.* In fact, both the president and the American people might be able to laugh the toxin and/or radioactivity away. . . . And surely getting the American people to increase their Laughter Quotients (LQs) might be as important as developing MX Missile Systems, Stealth Bombers, etc.

Within two weeks, Deaver responded with appreciation for my

> support for the manner in which this administration handled the encounter, [adding], I agree with your emphasis on the importance of humor and paradox in placing events in the proper perspective. Often a prescient and irreverent remark can do more than a mountain of serious studies . . .

Not long after, I wrote to James Watt, the controversial Secretary of the Interior, congratulating him for what might become the most important double paradox in American history; [namely], drill the oil; mess up the landscape, and there'll be little reason for people to use oil and cars to see the landscape. This in the long run may alleviate the oil shortage.

Day after day, in the spirit of H. L. Mencken, I scoured the media for cracks in the Establishment wall and expanded the list of recipients of such letters. When any event seemed totally preposterous, I tried to add fuel to the fire. When Pope John Paul II declared a Holy Year and the mayor of Rome was upset because the city didn't have facilities to accommodate a large number of pilgrims and expenses would be astronomical, I wrote to the pope proposing that the Vatican set up fifty to one hundred cots in the Sistine Chapel, rent them for $100/hour, and hence alleviate problems of both space and money, with a bonus: better viewing of Michelangelo's paintings. When the Vatican complained of deficit budgeting, I wrote to the Vatican comptroller suggesting that the pope stay home! In each instance I received very polite replies; but, fortunately, no request for contributions to the Vatican treasury!

When United Press International published an account of a university dean lured from Indiana to a state university in central Florida, incurring a $6,288.98 overrun for shipping 42,560 pounds of household goods (including a snowblade!), I suggested to the state comptroller that Florida might initiate awarding an outrage medal comparable to former senator William Proxmire's Golden Fleece Award for fiscal mismanagement. Within a week the chief of the Bureau of Auditing wrote me a serious note saying they were considering my suggestion, promising to notify me if the idea was adopted. More than two decades have passed and I've heard nothing. I'm wondering if the bureau is living up to its bureau-*crazy* reputation and still studying it? There's no surer way to kill an idea than to study it to death!

In the jestering mode I wrote both Senate and House members about provocative issues such as the administration's "disinformation" programs, secret arms deals with Iran, congressional pay raises, Reagan's rhetoric re: "winning a nuclear war," deterioration of faith in the American government, perpetuation of the "great Nixon" myth, and many other topics. Although I received routine replies to most of my letters, I sometimes felt like a jackass braying into an empty rain barrel; often the responses were non sequiturs. Obviously administrative assistants reached into the proverbial "circular file" to find a letter that might come close to a direct response. I could always hope, however, that somewhere on their mythical scoreboards that a vote had been recorded on any given issue.

My more recent exploration into the values of "jestereality" took the form of a full-length manuscript which records an experiment at a mythical Twain University. I appointed myself Campus Jester, complete with a contract requiring that I write a minimum of four letters per week for one academic year at a salary of $1/year more than the president's . . . a spoof in and of itself. Hence, for nine months I wrote the quota of letters, delving into every conceivable corner of this fictitious campus. Yet, I based the letters on my own half-century of life in academia, revealing its triumphs and tragedies, its fools and foibles, its idiocentric and conformists, its "brown-nosers" and dissenters, the full range of college and university activities. It covered the universal problems and proposed solutions of a typical campus. But the publishers to whom I sent it must have thought otherwise; I received some rejection slips to add to my bathroom walls. But this is to include samples of such jester efforts.

To: Robert Murview, Professor of Literature
Re: Medieval Literature 302

Dear Bob,

I took the liberty of peeking into your classroom on Tuesday, then tiptoed in and sat quietly in a back seat. I was enthralled as you moved the class painstakingly through an *explicatione de texte* of Beowolf's second encounter with the dragon, Grendel. You were articulate, clear, scholarly, and profound; however, since your voice was so strident, I wonder if you heard your *only* student in the class *snoring*?

　　Sincerely,

To: Roy Sands, Assistant Dean of Men

Dear Roy,

I'm glad you shared your plans for doing a book, titled *Innovative Alibis.* You are certainly at a vital university center for finding some of the best. I'll ask my daughter, a high-school teacher and dean of women, to keep her eyes open for some of the best examples she's encountered. Meanwhile, do you have the following:

- I didn't finish my degree for insufficient mourning for my dead poodle.
- On my way to class a limb fell off a tree and tore off my jeans.
- My period hit me at third period.
- My grandmother is planning to die next year; I'm thinking about it.

The introduction to your book, in the spirit of building up one's "treasury of merit," might suggest that these alibis are compiled for those expecting to commit "sins" or misdemeanors *in the future*.

Inexcusably yours,

To: James Battles, Director of Research and Grants
Re: Annual Festival of Fools

Dear Jim,

Many thanks for encouraging me by sending tips for applying for a Travel Grant to the Annual Festival of Fools in Amsterdam next year. I have solicited letters of recommendation from three (3) chairs. Word gets around, so I've now received thirty-three such letters from chairs and deans and seventeen from faculty members. Are they trying to tell me something?

Jesterly yours,

No question the jester has served an enormously important function in Western civilization, perhaps others, too. Actually no society can afford *not* to honor the jesting spirit even though they may kill jesters themselves. They serve as the conscience of a society and its subsets. Few people want to listen to the jester's perspectives, and those in positions of power may be the least likely to hear more than they want to hear. Yet, without freedom to send such letters to the media or those who control private organizations, we can hardly make our vaunted claims of living in a free society. Our stand-up comics, our cartoonists, some commentators or columnists such as Russell Baker and Dave Barry, may serve that function; but as yet, few if any are paid officially to tell the emperor: "You are naked!" Perhaps the day will come? And yet, one may be fairly certain that the power-hungry and egocentric persons in charge will find ways and means to blunt the ax, blur the image, feed *mis*-information into the pipeline, hence converting it into a sewer. While I still have my neck, it has been badly wrung at various times when my jester approach has been misinterpreted as a personal attack and drawn ad hominem fire in the form of the "nastiest" letters ever received in my academic life.

Hand-ling Foot-notes

A few decades ago I accepted the challenge of developing a handbook to guide Antioch's master's candidates through the process of earning a degree. After adding a few whimsical touches to the process and having sober-minded colleagues attempt to strike them from the text, I decided it should be called a *footbook*! We were certainly kicking the ideas around, in and out, and beyond all utility. Needless to say, I was outvoted. Hence, the title of this section.

Obviously, footnotes are a symbol of scholarly diligence and integrity so probably should be sacrosanct. They provide for reference, verification, and invitation for further scholarly exploration. Also they provide a gateway for meticulous and picayune persons to nitpick, keep the paper industry in business when footnoters consume forests of paper to explain, contradict, agree; also, to uncover fraud, suspicion, plagiarism, and other such practices. It is safe to assume that most footnotes are now mostly *end*notes, also that we've seen the end of most reading of them. Probably it is safe to say that fewer than 1 percent of them are ever read, probably that no more than 1 percent of that 1 percent are ever pursued to their origins.[12]

While "guilty" of "committing" many scholarly footnotes (possibly in this book?), I am perhaps most proud of a footnote associated with my student edition of the famous *Federalist*

Papers. It is commonly known that the authors, having been associated with the writing of the U.S. Constitution, reflected little trust in anybody in the newly proposed government. Hence, Alexander Hamilton, John Jay, and James Madison wrote the *Papers* to convince the people of the state of New York to ratify the document (hence the many checks and balances), *except*, in "No. 78," where one finds a rare trust in the judiciary . . . a trust that becomes the doctrine of judicial review as incorporated in the famous case *Marbury* v. *Madison* (1803). In my edition of the *Federalist*, "Footnote No. 98" reads as follows:

> At this point in the text Hamilton ran a footnote: "The celebrated Montesquieu, speaking of them [the judiciary] says: 'Of the three powers above mentioned, the judiciary is next to nothing. . . .' A close check of the Nugent text, which Hamilton used, reveals that Montesquieu actually said, 'Of the three powers above mentioned, the judiciary is *in some measure* next to nothing.' I have provided the italics to indicate that Montesquieu made a *qualified* judgment about the power of the judiciary, not an unqualified one, as Hamilton indicated. . . ."[13]

Those wishing to check this use of a critical footnote in American history are, of course, free to refer to the original texts. But three unanswerable questions remain: Why did Hamilton distort his appeal to Montesquieu? If Chief Justice John Marshall had not had the Hamiltonian justification for his position in launching the important doctrine of judicial review, what precedent might he have used for such a justification? And why did the editors of more than one hundred editions of the *Federalist Papers* before 1961 fail to discover this discrepancy? In short, footnotes need not necessarily be boring and/or irrelevant; or fluff in the determination of "truth" and "facts" in history. Those searching for adventures in unknown territory may wish to check out some of the sacred cows of our history to see if the footnotes on which they walk will hold them up. This task may be more difficult today than "once upon a time" since some documentation today finds writers merely alluding to a particular document without indicating the numbers of the pages where the data may be found. For a brief spoof on that process and its implications and perhaps some guidelines into the adventure, see my article on the topic in the *Chronicle of Higher Education*.[14]

The Search for Quotients

In this era of quantifying just about everything, it is hardly surprising to find that many aspects of living and human character are reduced to a quotient or an index. The most famous quotient is, of course, the IQ. As the first one to evolve in the course of developing human psychology, it has probably had the most use. But it is easy to conjure up a variety of other such quotients, such as the Perception Quotient, Listening Quotient, Romantic Quotient, etc. Once I wrote an editorial for the *Humanist* on the topic of "Change and Ostrich Quotients," i.e., the degree to which persons stick their heads in the sand when confronting world issues.[15] I suspect that there is a virgin field here since it's doubtful that all the wells of human motivation and character have been dipped dry. The re-FIRED adventurer might start where she stands, then expand imagination into every corner of endeavor from Best Activity at Times of Day (BAT-Q) to Zebraic Interests or Tendencies (ZITS-Q), i.e., preferences for striped clothing versus plaid and/or plain colors? The sky's the limit for developing thousands of scales. Then, too, the activity could be extrapolated to animal behavior, entomological observations, ad infinitum. After all, if an author were encourageed to write *Bug Haiku*,[16] why not extend observations, whimsicologies, and conclusions to the horizon?

Serious Needs to Be Playful

Persons coming this far in re-FIRE-ment ventures should have no difficulty extending interests and activities into other imaginative ones. All anybody needs to do is sit before a television set with blank paper and imagination to determine his humor quotient and the reasons for its growth and/or retardation. Then, being as objective as possible (since, after all, "objectivity is what I *say* it is"!), figure out the many ways that we can be serious about playfulness; why it sometimes works and why it doesn't. Reading Norman Cousins's *An Anatomy of an Illness,* apply Cousins's use of humor to become healthy to any illness you may have or even think you have! But it need not be confined to humor which you encounter. You can pursue many, many avenues for inventing play exercises that could evoke your joy of playing as a youth.

Spell Checks on the Computer

An unexpected source of humor and playfulness emerged from the Microsoft Spell Check on my computer. I stumbled onto it one day when checking a letter I'd written about the then House Speaker Newt Gingrich. Lo and behold! it came up on the screen as "jingoist." Not too much later I quoted T. S. Eliot in another letter, the suggested spelling was "elite." Checking something that contained Berea, Kentucky, a substitute for Berea was "beer." My name became "Roe Airfield"; my wife's name, Maryllyn, became "Marlin"; and our condo gatehouse became "ghettoize." Nixon's was "Nikon"! So many apt descriptions evolved from the proper names, I could not but wonder who had constructed this computerized dictionary? Was the connection between the Georgia congressman and jingoism conceived by a Democrat who did not like the House Speaker? And surely T. S. Eliot's poetry has been regarded as "elite" by more than one poetry critic. Also, gatehouses tend to ghettoize communities, albeit "golden ghettos" more frequently than ethnic. Are these serious questions or simply wordplay? Possibly the first Maryllyn in the world was a mermaid?

Fun Queries . . . Whimsicology

Those with computers may not only wish to join the several humor networks on the Internet, but more importantly contribute to them via storytelling, doggerel, and other modes of expression. Long before the Internet became popular, I developed two or three personal networks around the notion of whimsicology (the study and invention of humor as whim, not the kind involving arbitrary hurting of others).

I called one of my networks "Ocean River Boundless Group Organization" (ORB-GO) and one of the documents that I circulated, "Whimsicology 701," a course at the College of Hard Knocks. Among the topics and problems critiqued:

- If the mayor of Portville claims anything as a *fact*, divide by the square root of 20,422.945 to assess its true value;

- If the assessor of Portville promises to do anything favorable for its citizens, petition him *not* to do so since it's better that he do nothing than pretend to help;

- If the city government uses the word "empirical," quickly put on your rhyming hat and utter a mantra, "Hysterical, hysterical, hysterical. . . ."

- If the city claims to save us from anything—debt, thieves, worry, whatever—recite another mantra, "Save us from our saviors!"

To this network, I added SPOOF or the "Society for Proving Offbeat Observations for Fun" and occasionally broadcast a bulletin from Rocky Bottom in Maine (all coves are rocky in Maine!). I sent to this group of sole "souls" such bulletins as:

AN OUTLINE FOR MODIFYING INSTRUCTIONS
FOR SOFTWEAR IN THE OUTHOUSES OF AMERICA
    Activities at Dis-Union of Learning Ink (DULI)
    Where There's Sprung Hope there's no Wrench
    Advanced Whimsicological Ecology (AWE)
    Institute for the Study of Moral Pigmies (ISOMP)

It was also fun to distribute a memo, "Footnote to Scholarly Sources of Whimsicology," that included addresses of the Hug Club, Joy Germs Unlimited, International Save-the-Pun Foundation, World Humor and Irony Membership (WHIM), and the *Journal of Polymorphous Diversity.*

We also enjoyed exchanging dialogues with headlines; such dialogues date quickly, of course, but there's "no law against" reading the newspaper or newsmagazine, watching television and carrying on a conversation simultaneously with the anchorpersons who are dispensing the news. After all, if they can run a headline or lead sentence about the bombing of some distant city or describe in vivid detail the nature of a plane or bus crash with resulting deaths, why can't you ask questions you'd like answered, such as:

Why do you ask the spouse of a dead victim how she feels?

When will you report on more positive happenings in Tim Buc Tu?

Won't the committee study the recommendations to death? etc.

It's fun, too, making collages of cartoons or punch lines from comic strips. One called "WHIMSICOLLAGE," on standard-sized 8½" × 11" paper, consists of eleven interlocking articles and cartoons including brief articles on "Plan to Knock Hole in Northern Lights Fails," "Bare Residents Flee Nudist Camp Fire," and a Frank & Ernest cartoon in which one of the characters is asking the guru on a mountaintop, "All existence is a joke? You can't be serious!" Once again, as in so many fun things that can be done with everyday materials, use your imagination and the sky's the limit.

Then, too, if Harvard associates can sponsor the Annals of Improbable Research and award "Ig Nobel" prizes as spoofs to honor offbeat inventions,[17] why not look with favor upon various halls of shame? Think not only of those who follow conventional wisdom and are judged and perhaps are honored for best this or best that; think also of those who defy conventional prizewinning and judging. Prizes for the worst and/or the most mediocre might be fun to invent in the spirit of the Harvard "Ig

Nobels." Harvard and/or Berkeley and/or Tulane may eventually recognize Universities Without Walls for their contributions to both serious and absurd aspects of American life, hence fulfilling my humanistic fantasy.[18] But persons who have re-FIRED and cannot be "fired" from their jobs probably stand the best opportunities for writing grooks and haiku, do-it-yourself kits, or whimsicology pieces to stretch the mind and laughter muscles.

Words   with   a   Hue   (or   to   Hew?)

The pun is no new literary form. Shakespeare utilizes it in shaping Falstaff, one of his favorite characters, although plays on words add to the spice of many of his plays, both comedy and tragedy. Nor is it difficult to find hymns sung to the pun in contemporary writing. Richard Lederer, a teacher and columnist, for instance, who has been "looking at language" in newspapers and books for many years, contributed a regular column in the Portland, Maine, *Sunday Telegram*. He is not reluctant to solicit puns from readers and also entertains us with an admirer's "preying on words," such as

> What was Jonah wailing about?
> A minor's life is in the pits.
> Offal smells like it sounds.[19]

For some reason many people detest puns; but the irony is that whenever one is with a punster, everybody has a good time: the punster is in thirteenth heaven; the critic and one tending to "boo" is also having a good time. For years it's been my contention that it's a win-win form of wordplay. It's a wonderful lubrication for conversation and human interaction. The re-FIRING person, with fewer fears about economic survival and "what people will say," has every reason to develop the punning skill. He might wish to do it along with composing limericks where the ability to pun enhances the power of writing in that vogue.

Highways to Laughter

Somewhere around 1980, much public relations swirled around Gov. Jim Rhodes of Ohio when he erected arches over a major highway at the Ohio-Pennsylvania line. They were costly and seemingly glitzy at a time when money was anything but plentiful.

Being none too enamored of Governor Rhodes anyway, the first time I saw one of the arches, in a split second I wrote:

> Half a zero
> in a state
> that counts
> on its fingers . . .

Shortly thereafter I started a journal that I called *Half a Zero . . . or a Compendium of Whimsicology*, dedicated "To Laughter." As I traveled around the country, I collected whimsical notions and observations in the belief that laughter may be our last best cope. My collection included some of the following:

Acronyms

EROS—Era of the Rip-off Syndrome
REAM—Reagan Era for Advancement of Millionaires
CIA—Committee of Idiocy Associates

FUN-ny Names

Jacky Ickx—Belgian race driver
Candy Pees—Interviewed on TV in Miami
Marge Pickle—*Miami Herald* obit
True Sleeper—from a *Portland Press Herald* obit
Rita Birdsong married to Donald Branch

Then from a Yarmouth, Nova Scotia, phone book, the following surnames:

Bastarache, Tudball, Kruckle, Oikle, Tidd, Woodover, Outhouse (all thirty-three of them), van Tassel, etc.

License plate "numbers" observed

HO HO HO; JET-1; KEEWEE; FOG; RANCH; MOM-P; DINGBAT; GO NANA; HOLLY B; REALM; BOATYARD; GO FOR IT; BAS-1; GRAIN; RATLA; MOI; KORO, to say nothing about radio-station numbers and codes—you name it, and you'll find it. Collecting such "numbers" is a delightful occupation for children on long automobile trips. But adults, too, can join the game by speculating on what type of person might choose such vanity tags . . . and also wonder, too, about some numbers which made it past the censor hurdles that exist at the state license bureau-*crazies*? Is this free speech at best? or worst? or something in between? In short, these become triggers for both short and extensive dialogues, even laughter on the highways.

More Words with Hues or to Be Hewn

Semiversal, methodology, mundanities, metadamn, minilithic, trivia borealis, Hobohemia, castrophize, medi*evil,* media-okra-ty, sychophats, psychophants, and so on . . .

While it's not so easy to piece "chunks" of words together in English, as it is in German for instance, the sky's the limit, simply playing with compounding and double-compounding words. A similar process, though in reverse of compounding words, is to take a multisyllable word or phrase, tear it apart, and bounce it around as follows: mysticism . . . miss tism . . . mist-is-"sm" . . . misty is "mmm" . . . mis-'tis-sim, and so on. Or try saying aloud: earning a living, learning a living, learning and giving, giving and learning, giving and living, giving and learning, earning and learning, learning and earning. . . . Repeat it rapidly! Then, try messing up common expressions to concoct such combinations as "Sodom and Gonorrhea."

Of course, you can collect your own favorite quotes; don't worry about competing with Bartlett; he just happened to get here before you did. Also, you can invent your own "quotes" and never have to bother to put marks around them, such as:

Damn the soldier ants, full speed ahead.

Let's go snap beans and a few words.

Moving is bringing things together just as they're falling apart.

Siamese twins: a joint enterprise.

We need fewer ironmasters and more ironymasters in this world.

In this plastic era tomatoes are grown for market to be picked but not eaten.

They went to Beijing to have a Pe(a)(e)king experience.

The retired hermit in Switzerland might rightly be called: Alps Hermeritus.

Questions with a Hue!

Just as the half-life of a question may stimulate other queries and perspectives, so may idle queries such as:

Does your secretary black out when using white-out?
What part of "NO" don't you understand?
Does celebration recapitulate cerebration?
Where's the parrot in paradox?
. . . or even an ox in fox?
. . . who took the whim out of whimsy?
. . . or the tug from tuggle?
. . . and ugh in struggle?

More Pun-Americanism

He was shot down by a small boor.
Humans cannot live by dread alone.
He got off a series of one-scenters.
Fiction was readily available.
He competed with Steinbeck by writing *The Gripes of Wrath*.
He lost the pulse in his feet, so aged in vein.

In the spirit of Oedipus and Lear, he fought for a guaranteed annual rage.

Sounds and Furies

Just as children love poems and expressions which rhyme or will roll off their tongues, anybody is capable of wordplay which fills the needs that children have. Try these aloud:

> High humidity
> quick liquidity
> clear lucidity
> quid pro quidity . . .

> Diddly pooh
> piggly doo
> kitty ding
> and owly hoo!

Book and Film Titles

You, too, can invent your own book and film titles, such as: *Unremembered Dreams, Undigested Learning, Indigestible Humor, Distance as Illusion, Come with the Wind, The Stars Look Big-Bangward*, etc. There is no end of such fun, either by yourself or with family and friends. Best of all, if you keep your own records, you have complete control of the "parse" strings.

Family Expressions

Is there a family which doesn't have closetsful of favorite expressions, both sharable and unsharable? It's a mark of creative and collective family memory to gather them once, twice, ten times before they fade away with the passing of each generation. Because . . . when they do, it's nearly impossible to gather them for any purpose or for any amount of money. My dad was not a poet, but he was a wordmonger and sang ditties and chanties morning, noon, and night. In later life he always greeted me with Joe Penner's expression, "Whooooo, *me*?" Hence, collecting them upon his death was a "duty" that I enjoyed. He spoke of very old persons as living "longer than a crowbar," old tumbledown houses as "leaning toward Sawyers." One of my sisters persisted in asking, "Where's Sawyers?" And he didn't know! He loved to give names to friends who came to his garage: Charles Lamb was Sheep; Reed was Long Blade of Grass. Sometimes expressions usually used in tight family situations burst into public light in embarrassing ways. One family member, attending a sewing circle of rather conservative college faculty women, became frustrated about something going backward so she said, "You got it bassackward." And not until a hush came over the group did she realize what she had said. She'd heard that expression used by her mother and grandmother hundreds of times. We obtain these stories all too infrequently, and, when we do, there's a tendency to put the lid on them.

Exercise No. 10: "Well! Fan Me with a Brick!"

My neighbor, Debbie Goebel, tells of her mother, Evelyn, using this expression when hearing something surprising about another person. As noted in my own case, every family is filled with such favorite expressions. Search into your own family history and compile a list and include the persons you associate with such expressions. When do you use them? How do they serve to perpetuate family traditions, culture, loyalty, and identity? Which can you use in any situation? Particular situations? Find the oldest person in your extended family and discover what they can tell you about such expressions. Compare notes with your siblings and friends.

Next we'll examine the value of listening beyond the words, asking questions and using the Internet more intelligently, appreciating the value of Zen, and "closing circles" by converting wonder into letters to the dead.

Notes

1. "To Achieve Success, Try Failure," *Boston Globe*, June 15, 1999.

2. A variation of Paul Tillich's *The Courage to Be* (New Haven, Conn.: Yale University Press, 1952).

3. Parker Palmer, *The Courage to Teach* (San Francisco: Jossey-Bass, 1998), pp. 62–63.

4. Humor from Net, "The Facts of Life" by Joseph R. Kinel, August 9, 1997.

5. Pico Iyer, "The Eloquent Sounds of Silence," *Time* (January 25, 1993).

6. *Baltimore Sun*, February 15, 1997.

7. Roy P. Fairfield, *Seaside Fables and Other Incites* (Saco, Maine: Bastille Books, 1994), foreview.

8. Those familiar with graphic arts and James Thurber's *Further Fables for Our Time* may detect the way in which I "borrowed" concepts from M. C. Escher and Thurber. From the great etcher, the notion of a checkerboard landscape metamorphosing into a life of its own; from Thurber, the notion of a moon with black and yellow stripes.

9. *Saco Valley Cookery* (Kearney, Nebr.: Morris Press, 1998), p. 97.

10. Bertrand Russell, "A New Decalogue," *New York Times Magazine,* December 16, 1951.

11. For Models, visit Baker Library, Dartmouth College, and study José Orozco's famous murals.

12. Are you a part of those percentages?

13. Roy P. Fairfield, ed.,*The Federalist Papers* (Garden City, N.Y.: Doubleday Anchor, 1961), p. 302.

14. Roy P. Fairfield, "The Implications of Pageless Documentation (3: 1939–1979)," *Chronicle of Higher Education* (May 5, 1982): 24.

15. Roy P. Fairfield, "Change and Ostrich Quotients," *Humanist* 28, no. 4 (1968): 2.

16. J. W. Hackett, *Bug Haiku* (Tokyo: Japan Publications, 1968). See also footnotes on haiku books, chapter 6.

17. *Biddeford & Saco* (Maine) *Journal-Tribune*, October 9, 1998.

18. In one of my more discouraged moments, when watching the original vision for the creation of Universities Without Walls go down before the bulldozers of conformity and the shocking power of accreditors, I wrote a prospectus for a University Without Balls. It was easy to see why traditional institutions might applaud such a university rather than one dedicated to person-centered learning.

19. Roy Couch, a friend, granted permission via phone, July 26, 1999.

CHAPTER 5

Beneath the Bottom Line

The creative temperament and process virtually demands that the creator perceive from many, even odd, angles of vision, and remain open in order to stretch beyond conventional wisdom, past the jaundiced view that reveals little or nothing. Actually children who ask mother, "Who created God?" or "Who was God's daddy and mommy?" probably reflect both the logic and air of wonder more at two years of age than ever again. When parents forestall the answer to those questions with nonanswers that take them "off the hook," they neglect the fact that there may be something beneath the bottom lines! Unfortunately, that one gesture or nonanswer may close a door leading to "who knows where?" In this country we all too frequently convert such an accounting description into a metaphor with wide-ranging implications. When one uses the "bottom-line" metaphor, presumably that stops all further inquiry. This is dangerous stuff when openness is the attitude required for creative endeavor, whether that endeavor involves graphics, musical scales, poetic possibilities, theatrical or ballet movements, corporate structures and processes, or the patience and skill to create a wonder-producing needlework masterpiece.

Creative Polyphrenia/ Multiple Awareness

There's ample evidence of multiple states of consciousness, dating back to prehistoric tribal dances and trances and the yen for Zen. Since Greek times, too, Western civilization has been entranced by oracles such as the Delphic Oracle, Socrates' muse, and a dozen variations of "the Orphic Voice." In modern times psychologists, parapsychologists, and neurophysicists, obscure, condemned, and famous, have attempted to delineate modes of consciousness, subconsciousness, and unconsciousness. Both famous and infamous researchers and experimenters have delved into the impact of mind-expanding natural and synthetic materials upon consciousness and human functioning. Robert Graves, perhaps the most famous romantic poet of the twentieth century, experimented with such substances as well as flirting with his poetic muses (both in ideal and in physical female form) for half a century. Skeptics may confirm this by reading his *White Goddess.* As a recent biographer observed, Graves "believed that the best poems are written in a suspended state of 'glamour-trance' and 'mushroom visions' . . . ."[1] His life and creative muse depended upon writing under the inspiration of several "white goddesses," a feeling I attempted to intensify in a poem, "Transformation":[2]

> White shadows
> no matter her
> height
>   color
>   or weight
> she cast a white shadow
> aura
>   glaze

over the poet's eyes
though his other self
cries with grief
over length of human life
the reaper's knife
as sharp and certain
as a pendulum's swing
but the white shadow
with more momentum
than any other influence
that sings. . . .

But what does this have to do with the "average person" who feels a spark of creativity in her bones? One is, of course, free to experiment with substances, keeping in mind the known legal limitations and/or risks. Since much has been written and spoken about the topic, one is free to "listen" to the experience of others. But having spent a half century writing various kinds of documents (from bureau-*crazy* reports to fiction to fables to poetry to tens of thousands of letters), I can attest to the phenomenon of trance. Writing in the dark (described in chapter 2) promotes a state of being that enhances free-flowing or process writing, insight via no sight! Dreaming enables a person to tap into another state of awareness; and when dreams are recorded in some way, a person has evidence of their "other state." Daydreaming also provides everybody the "space" for sensing the world graphically, verbally, orally, and otherwise in ways not normally bounded by the ordinary laws of physics. Modern painters, sculptors, and musicians have enabled us to perceive "reality" from several angles of vision, sometimes several angles simultaneously—as Picasso and his bewildering "offspring" have made dramatic. Likewise with the music of Igor Stravinsky and John

Cage. In short, as in physics where Einstein made "the relativity of simultaneity" acceptable, the same concept/phenomenon is possible in everyday-life-become-articulate in some creative form.

My "return" to poetry (other than the situational "roses-are-red" genre) challenged my own self-credibility. During twenty years of traditional teaching of history and the social sciences, I had taken and used most words and English syntax quite literally/conventionally, only gaining some freedom from that straitjacket via modern histories of painting and music. But I threw off the straitjacket in a strange and unsuspected way. While directing a teacher-training master's program for Antioch College in Putney, Vermont, we faculty and students constructed our own curriculum. We believed that it was perfectly legitimate to hold our own "film festivals," viewing as many as four or five films per night for a week at a time, films which one of our learners borrowed directly from the Canadian Film Board. The number of experimental films was legion and in the film "language" of the day "blew our minds." For some unknown reason I felt the urge to watch such films with a yellow legal pad on my lap; and as the images poured out in great cataracts, so did words via which I metamorphosed *the experience into personal knowing and expression.* I sometimes filled a half-dozen pages of scribbling per film; these became a verbal record of my own inner film which I could read to appreciate or manipulate into poetic form, a process available to everybody.

While in the midst of those freeing processes, I was returning home from a New York City educational meeting along the Massachusetts interstate, driving at 70 mph at midnight, close to being in a highway trance, when a poem "wrote itself." I was determined to "capture" it; hence, upon crossing the border into Vermont, I pulled into the Welcome Area to record it while it was fresh so I might intensify the experience. No other person or car was in sight, so I parked, pulled out a pad of paper, and wrote:

Harlem or Hanoi . . .

We roar down
a corridor of lights
through night
so black
I
see doom
our probable destiny . . .

over Hanoi
or Harlem
with napalm
and indifference
to inflict
our wounds . . .

While writing that poem at the side of the interstate, the following thoughts flashed through my mind:

Here I am . . . a white male . . . dressed in a proper suit . . . what shall I say if a cop stops to ask what I'm doing? Should I tell him the Frost story about not being admitted to a fraternity until he told his prospective "brothers" that he took walks in the forest to "chew the bark off the trees"? Or what if I were a black male or little old Chicano lady and a cop came along, could I avoid being carried to jail if I told the authorities that I was "writing poetry"?

That was a watershed moment. I came to trust my "muse," my process, my parallel consciousness, or call it what I might. During the next ten years, while engaged in operating or founding new graduate programs, I experimented with various means of experiencing more than one level of consciousness simultaneously. During long and sometimes dreary committee meetings, I used my yellow pad to scribble down the left-hand side the contents of *what* was being said; down the right-hand side I wrote haiku, grooks (doggerel), free verse, and doodles. Sharing these processes with my learners, they observed that I might be using the right and left sides of my brain concurrently or at least symbolically.

Also during this time I evolved skills in writing the haiku and grooks presented in chapter 6. In addition, I perfected the technique of writing in the dark, felt more familiar with the use of metaphors, developed the skill (however dangerous) of writing poetry on the carseat beside me while driving and listening to the radio. There were times when it seemed fairly clear that I was "working" on at least three levels of consciousness: I was driving the car, listening to words or music, and writing poetry in my head. At the end of that decade, approximately in the mid-1970s, I was striving to reach four to six levels of brain activity. I may even have damaged some of the neurons in my brain when I tried to stretch that far—but all without substances.

A major conclusion: with some discipline and the willingness to be open, there *is no bottom line*. The "bottom-line" metaphor is deceiving and so superficial that it's hardly worth using.

An Anatomy of Dissent

Important, too, in the evolution of my consciousness and my confidence in human potential was my study and writing about dissent in America. I developed a book-length manuscript on the history and function of dissent in this country. Our official constitutional and Supreme Court histories encourage individual expression which gives a wide latitude to dissenting opinions. We have dozens of mature institutions, such as the American Civil Liberties Union and the Anti-Defamation League, organized to guarantee dissent. Also, there are ongoing battles over such issues as free expression by hate-generated groups such as the Ku Klux Klan over dissent. In fact, it's a rare year when some one of these issues and/or incidents do not crowd other news off CNN or reach the Supreme Court.

During the late 1960s and early 1970s, student dissent occupied much of my interest and time. I read numerous books on the topic and wrote reviews about them for various journals. I even spent an academic quarter at the University of California at Berkeley studying the Free Speech Movement firsthand as well as participating in teach-ins there and at Columbia University. These efforts integrated my essential humanism as well as my career-long teaching of freedom issues and the evolution of person-centered learning modalities at Antioch College and the Union Graduate School. I learned the challenges and dangers of working for a cause; especially the dangers of being a "true believer." Yet, as a person on the liberal/liberating side of the fence, I learned about the ironies and paradoxes of promoting dissenting views, especially the paradox of intense work for the liberal position without becoming doctrinaire. I also learned about the dangers of "political correctness." Being an AARP member, for instance, can be both a boon and a bane for the independent-minded dissenting humanist, but at least one can stand his ground and avoid being a mugwump or fence-sitter! What one creates for a position or attitude as a basis for action can be an ongoing process of revision.

The Self-Deceiving Prophecy Revisited 2[3]

How easy it is to misuse a tool or even find a creative way to use one differently than the inventor intended. Put an eating implement in the hands of a child and watch him find his mouth! Such was the social-scientific tool that Robert Merton invented in 1949 when writing his insightful essay, "The Self-Fulfilling Prophecy," discussed in chapter 2. Since then, it has become almost a household phrase. Merton focused on the "moral alchemy" that in-groups use to denigrate out-group persons and behavior. In short, he added, "the right activity by the wrong people becomes a thing of contempt, not of honor." Hence, those in power continue to control, and passive persons too frequently accept the denigration that contributes to their fate as "victims." As I contend at greater length, the tool, "self-fulfilling prophecy," especially as used by the humanistically inclined, has come to be associated with "fulfillment" or self-fulfillment, an essentially positive notion. But the other side of the coin suggests that it is too frequently used with negative connotations and denotations, self-deceiving impacts.

It is worthwhile to speculate that the essential nature of experience may be self-deception, depending upon any particular view of "reality." And while social mores, educational emphases, and the billion images that the media provide may create norms that we come to accept as "reality," we know that there are millions upon millions of other angles of vision. Nor can any of us feel too comfortable when perceived by others as deceiving or self-deceiving. Whether we are contemplating author Gertrude Stein's observation that "a rose is a rose is a rose" or dealing with a local ordinance that defines "junkyard," we know that language usually conditions perception. And if somebody says, "That's a junkyard," and I see it as an "auto dismantling industry," I'm likely to be written off as "crazy." An artist, creating a piece of sculpture from old auto parts, assembled in the shape of a "human," may be able to "get away" with his definitions; yet, unless he has created something that "never was on land or sea," his work is likely to be eschewed rather than sought, be banned by the authorities in control! He has violated the norm; he has deceived himself, but he probably cannot "deceive" those who abide by the norms. After all, they *know* what *reality* is!

Charging another person with self-deception is tricky business. But the potential creator of an artifact, a process, an institution, even in the glow of self-fulfillment, may have honest doubts about self-deception. And at the point of social interaction he may wish to ask himself the consequences of his creative efforts. In short, ask, "Have I gone beyond the bottom line, and what difference does it make?"

The Paradox of Freedom

As outlined in my essay "Freedom Is Frightening,"

> The voices of freedom have sounded in many tones and tongues though the centuries. . . . The central themes of these cries (from Pericles to the Declaration) are summed up in the American Bill of Rights and other manifestoes, but might well be stated as freedom *from* encroachments of government and private endeavors upon individual and community choosing, as well as freedom *to,* and the responsibility *for* choosing what is best for the health of body and mind.[4]

In short, freedom is a complex privilege or right; and, despite the history of the fight for whatever kind of freedom, it's appropriate to ask why freedom is so elusive. It's not difficult to perceive the struggle as counteracting the action of a mighty stream of authoritarians of every kind, from the so-called benevolent kings to the most repulsive of dictators, from the impact of a Roman culture devoted to "bread and circuses" to one devoted to mindless television. Surely the list of external opponents is legion. But it is equally if more complexly related to human habits, wishes, and potential for self-deception. Psychologist Erich Fromm's *Escape from Freedom* is a landmark in understanding why freedom is frightening, also a kind of blueprint for tracing group anxieties. Or as the comic-strip character Pogo once observed, "We have met the enemy and they is us." The obvious existence of many cults and movements reflect a widespread psychological need for many to escape from freedom. At some ultimate point, one may use Ernest Becker's "denial of death" as a metaphor and apply it to the kind of living which is a daily dying![5]

As suggested many times in this volume, I've consistently and insistently encouraged freedom of choice throughout my teaching and writing, basing my urging upon historical and constitutional precedent as well as experience and "faith" in individuals. Institutionally, I've allied myself with frontier-type organizations such as the Peace Corps, experiential learning modalities, and building new hiking trails, both literally and metaphorically. Yet in frequently asking associates/students/learners, "Why is it so difficult to choose?" answers have come back: "It's frightening"; "I've had no preparation for it"; "Our society gives only lip service to it." Others argue, "I'm fearful of the consequences." And, of course, the latter have much evidence to support such a view. Sheep are rarely slaughtered individually; not so some of our mythical heroes such as Socrates, Tom Paine, and Galileo! It has been painful for me, as coinventor of various graduate programs on the learning frontiers, to watch accreditors squeeze some of the freedom dimensions from person-centered learning modalities. Or participants themselves forfeit "freedom to choose" while seeking "certainty." With urbanization, technocrization, industrialization and bureacratization of our society at full momentum, even with the Internet, it is not easy to deal with the welter of choices before us. Perhaps the greatest challenge for teachers working with youth as well as seniors seeking knowledge and experience via Elderhostel, cruise lectures, and other forms of "returning to school" is attempting to encourage others to master the art of choosing and to do it with creative verve and satisfaction. But, as I concluded my essay "Freedom Is Frightening" two decades ago, "One hopes the vision of the future will, perhaps, maximize human freedom and the quality of life. But, . . . we'll have to work like hell to achieve it!"

The Half-Life of a Question

Since scientists such as Marie and Pierre Curie did the original research on radium and radiation experts began calculating the half-life of physical elements, the world has become increasingly familiar with the *concept* of various natural phenomena having half-lives. Yet most folk probably do not know that the fallout from a nuclear bomb contains all kinds of radioactivity, some with very short half-lives and some with longer ones. By now all should know that nuclear night would probably result from an all-out nuclear war. This may be dramatized by observing that carbon 14 has a half-life of five thousand years; that is, it would take another five thousand years to lose what was then life, and so on . . . in short, about sixty thousand years to decay completely.

We have come to understand, too, that the half-life of an idea or a body of knowledge can be both short and long. Surely, the kind of knowledge one encounters in a radio or quiz show is short.

Closer to home one need only play the game Trivial Pursuit to understand one's own half-life of memory. In the field of administration, it is little wonder that words such as "administrivia" are coined to emphasize the half-life of insights, processes, and practices in that field. No doubt each field of human endeavor has its specialist in such half-lives. Come to think of it, museums memorialize and preserve selected artifacts and data in an attempt to maintain some semblance of the half-life that remains. We know the major museums and their work to keep memories of the arts fresh, but what do we know of minor museums such as Sally Bennett's, in South Florida? She has been working and collecting for decades to start a Big Band Hall of Fame Museum. Will her effort preserve the half-life of that era of the twentieth century associated with that particular kind of music?[6]

Such questions lead to a different type of query; namely, what is the half-life of a question? It's one thing to ask about material elements, quite another to inquire about more ephemeral data or experience. If I am asked, "How was dinner at the Sheridan last evening?" who cares if the particular question is irrelevant in twenty seconds, in two days, or ever? Likewise, who *really* wants an answer to the oft-asked question, "How are you feeling?" And how long is the question relevant?

Possibly it trivializes the basic question about ideas to ask some of these questions; yet to study them certainly raises questions about fundamental curiosity.

I contend that we could learn much about most fields of endeavor and most cultures if we focused on the half-life of questions. For instance, the question that Plato poses at the outset of *The Republic*, "What is justice?" is as vital today as it was twenty-five centuries ago; but should the earth exist sixty thousand years from now, will the query about justice survive? Likewise other philosophical questions that provide the basis of philosophical and cultural observations the world over, for instance: What is truth? self? reality? being and Being? consciousness? Probably no creative person can fail to ask such questions, though not necessarily all of them. How can a person feel or know that she is creative without asking questions about the process of querying?

Literature, painting, sculpture, dance, computer software design, math, science, a new sailor's knot, in short most human endeavor addressing humans-in-the-universe concern such creativity. This is not to say that everyday experience is unimportant; probably the quality and quantity of such consciousness involves questions whose half-life is relatively short. Survival depends upon it. Yet, this does not negate my contention that the creative impulse and the consequences of its being played out are, indeed, worth considering in the context of half-life querying.

It is, of course, common knowledge that it is not only the *what* of a question (and its half-life) but also the *how* and *why* a question is asked that either advances or retards inquiry. Surely the question "Are you hungry?" rarely competes with "What is the nature of the universe?" But a question such as "How are you adjusting to your diabetic condition?" might have life-and-death implications. The creative questioner or *live*-er would hardly mix such questions although an inventor of a new ritual or liturgy might attempt to blend the three. We do know that many misunderstandings grow from failure to know when a question is appropriate. We also know that some questions can be life-threatening if the purpose of the question is to denigrate or challenge another person's integrity or fundamental assumptions. Also, if the other person is expected to change her way of living or being.

Exercise No. 11: Your Queries

Make a list of questions that you regard as trivial, with a very short half-life.

Make a similar list of those that might have a half-life of a year, five years. Also, what personal questions have endured throughout your life, birth to the present?

How do you distinguish between long-lived (so called "eternal" questions) and those that may live for only a single lifetime? What difference does it make to the creative person?

What current social, economic, and political questions do you see that will have a half-life of five years, twenty-five? Can you conceive of a "utopian" model of society that would change the half-life of such questions?

In a Miami lecture the novelist Chaim Potok spoke of asking questions at 4 A.M. They kept him awake since they dealt with matters of life and death, so he called them Four O'Clock Questions. Do you have them? If so, why are they important?

Favorite Unasked Questions

It's a rare person with 20/20 hindsight who has not wished that he had asked a crucial question in an important dialogue, meeting, or social situation. Failure to ask such a question might serve as an illustration of Sigmund Freud's superego, censor-in-action observations. Who has not pondered "the difference" it might have made, *to ask or not to ask?* in one's career, in personal relationships with another, in one's personal growth, and so on? At this juncture, perhaps another exercise will highlight the relevance of this line of querying.

Exercise No. 12: Lost Questions

Upon reflection, make a list of a half-dozen questions you wish you'd asked at some crucial points in your life. How old were you at the time? Can you remember *why* you did *not* ask them? Can you speculate about the consequences if you had?

Can you concoct a scenario relating to your current work or personal life situation wherein you'd like to ask questions you have never asked? Write them down so you may refer to them at a later time and determine whether or not you've asked them, what difference it made? or might make if you *dare* do it in the future?

Make a list of questions you wish you had asked some member of your family, questions which nobody else could possibly answer.

In the same spirit, make a list of famous people (of any era) with whom you wish you might have dialogued. Then write to at least one of them or make a tape recording of your side of the conversation. You could use any number of Plato's dialogues as models for such a conversation, or consult Ira Progoff, a Jungian psychologist who wrote guidelines for such dialogues.[7]

Upon completion of such an exercise, reflect upon what you learned. Make a point of discussing it with your spouse, other family member, trusted friend.

At some time in an apt context, especially in a classroom, corporate training session, or tight emotional situation, ask the LEADER the following question:

What Is *Your* Favorite *Unasked* Question?

As soon as possible, describe in writing what happened. In cases where I've asked this question *publicly*, I have been both surprised and inspired by the responses. In one instance involving an internationally known person, the man was exceedingly humble, repeated the question, took at least a minute or two to respond, then said he'd not had such an experience before. In another instance where I'd seen an authoritarian type bullying (and BS-ing) his way through a question-and-answer period following a lecture, he "showed his stripes" by saying that he'd never faced such a question and saw no value in doing it. Bullies and insecure speakers have threatened and/or attempted to humiliate and intimidate me. This man did not! Possibly, you may never know how much you can learn about human personality and the half-life of a question until you take such a creative approach to querying.

Zen and the Art of Hustling

Since the appearance of such books as *Zen in the Art of Archery* and *Zen and the Art of Motorcycle Maintenance*,[8] it seems possible to approach almost any activity from a Zen angle of vision/feeling/consciousness of consciousness. In fact, when I dreamed up this subheading in making an outline for this book, I didn't have the slightest idea of what I might say about "Zen and the Art of Hustling." I thought it might be fun to invent the topic, then at some later date see what it might lead to. It is now "somewhat later," so, let's see . . .

Beginning with Webster: we find three definitions of the verb "hustle":

1. To shake together in confusion; to push, jostle, or crowd rudely.
2. To force onward rapidly; as he *hustled* the work.
3. To move or act with resolute energy.

Then, as a noun, Webster says, "one who hustles . . . a pushing or shoving." The last three of the four definitions are designated as "colloquial."

In each of these situations there is movement, much as archery, tennis, and maintaining motorcycles require movement. And, indeed, the typical (and/or stereotypical) hustler in today's economic world (regardless of the medium) is one who is attempting to move the sale of automobiles or other goods, services such as insurance, salvation via television, or some other kind of illusion (see chapter 8 on illusion). To use other clichés: they are selling hope rather than soap, sometimes "soul" to sole souls who have already settled on the nature of their "soul," faith without conscience, etc. Usually, the terms "hustler" or "hustling" carry a pejorative connotation for those who do not approve of this method of selling; yes, selling or economic activity is usually involved although the process spills over into every form of human endeavor. And yet, I have heard both respected and respectful people explain and even justify what they were doing as "hustling." Frequently, too, as with Tennessee Williams's Willie Loman in the play *Death of a Salesman,* we've all heard that explanation permeated with despair. We know the tragedies of the Willie Lomans.

But what does "the art of hustling" require from Zen? Superficially, it seems to demand little more than is required when hitting the bull's-eye in archery. Just as a puritan must become a "moral athlete"[9] to survive until tomorrow, the hustler must develop his momentum (of speech, belief in product, psychological savvy, political know-how and know-when, etc., running the entire gamut of human activity) without too much thought or concern about ethics, how others may think of his activity or competence, or whether any specific "sale" is successful. Again, it's a matter of *thoughtless momentum*, something like putting our brain into neutral and letting the tongue wag on. As definitions go, "he's hustling the work." He's pushing and shoving. He's moving. And just as the archer must not think about hitting the target, the hustler must *not* think about his quota, his persona, his objectives, or whether or not he is jostling or rude. He'll be more successful by trying less hard—the essential paradox of Zen. Perhaps the most creative thing that he can consciously *do* is pick up and read (reread?) Eugen Herrigal's *Zen in the Art of Archery* and/or enroll in Zen classes or programs. After that, he must simply trust the process and become so "mindless" that at the end of any given day when he goes off "automatic pilot" and returns to his home and family, he may have to work diligently to reconstruct the meaning of his day's sales figures. A TV or talk-show "salvation salesman" might not even recognize himself on the tube or radio. In many respects he will not be the same person in reflection that he was in the act of hustling. If he thinks about greed's fueling his momentum, he may find the tank empty.

Scary stuff? Yes and no! Yes, for those who believe in or wish to perceive integrated and consistent personalities. No, for the hustler who may, though not necessarily, live in two relatively distinct worlds. Public "trials" of the TV evangelists in the 1980s reflected that split. Clinical psychologists might call it schizophrenia at its extreme. Everyday folk might perceive it as skill in living in separate compartments. A creative cynic might point out that it's easier to live in this world if one has at least three mutually exclusive sets of values, one for Monday, Wednesday, and Friday (like university course taking); another for Tuesday, Thursday, and Saturday; and a third for Sundays. And perhaps to be truly successful, a fourth set; namely, one for day and another for night. In short, there is plenty of room to practice Zen in four different areas, "pushing and shoving" at different levels of consciousness without much concern for one another. The genuine, Zen-focused hustler could conceivably become highly skilled in each subpersonality. Those observing her from the outside might call the behavior bizarre or morally corrupt (depending upon the criteria for morality), but the hustler might never know the difference. We have ample films that demonstrate the phenomenon of multiple personalities (e.g., *The Three Faces of Eve*). Stare long enough at a kaleidoscope, a white-on-white painting, a computer graphic, or a set of the great Dutch etcher M. C. Escher's etchings, and lo and behold it is transformed into something else! Who is to say that Zen cannot apply to the art of hustling?

Zen and Other Arts

In a dust jacket for David Brazier's book, *Zen Therapy: Therapy Transcending the Sorrows of the Human Mind*, D. T. Suzuki is quoted:[10]

> The "I" seems to be harassed in every way all day, and it feels constricted, inhibited, fearful of acting in the way it likes, and depending upon outsiders all the time for directions. What is this "I" that resents all these oppressions from without, revolting, complaining, irritated, upset, despondent, wavering, unable to be decisive? When you

ask a question in the Zen sense of the term, you must feel somewhere deep within yourself another "you" or "I" who is really above these psychological annoyances. Zen wants you to put your finger on this "I"....[10]

While Suzuki's perspective may be chosen for specific application to the therapeutic field, I think that it is fundamental to every human endeavor that requires a person to understand and feel comfortable with the "I" so central to one's being. To return to Herrigal's archery analogy, it requires great trust to aim the arrow without aiming it! Likewise one must trust in the trust assuming "automatic pilot" at some point while painting, composing musical scores, writing poems, sculpting, practicing medicine, teaching a class, choreographing a dance, or researching in some far-out region of the physical and/or biological universe. Then, too, trust in the trust!

Postage Due

How frequently we regret that we didn't converse with family members or friends before they died! When it's too late, we remember that we'd intended to ask that person for information or insights that we know she carried to her grave. One faces that void with mixed emotions, but with the clearest sense of dread about what it means to be too late. It's a flirtation with forever. Also resignation in having "closed the physical circle" on that relationship, but not the psychological. One "solution" to that dilemma: write letters to the dead.

This is to share a few paragraphs from letters I have written to people both famous and ordinary, between Mozart, Gandhi, and FDR on the one hand and my grandmother on the other:

Dear Amadeus,

As I write, I am listening to your Concerto #21 (did you count them, too?) ... it's snowing outside and a fireplace is burning inside; calm, the silence in cadence with your long slow violin and harpsichord passages, climbing into peaceful meadows. Perhaps such listening is the lifeblood, the very heart of vacations from our cacophonous world. Without such quiet moments, it might be difficult to understand or savor other moments ... something like the silence between notes. Thank you for having graced the earth ... for our grace.

Dear M. K. Gandhi,

It makes me want to cry to learn that your sons and daughters have abandoned your social and political prescriptions and your memory. Imagine! only six (6) universities with any courses in Gandhi Studies! And I want to scream from the rooftops, "Why have they forsaken you? and your teachings?" When I was growing up in the thirties, your tiny sheet-clad figure made more news on the front pages than some of the local elite. My family and I held our breaths during your encounter with the British troops. It didn't seem possible that your philosophy of satyagraha or civil disobedience could possibly wilt the soldiers as you looked down their gun barrels.

Dear FDR,

I apologize for having been so long writing to you. I am not sure how much my delay relates to my guilt of having grown up in an unreconstructed Maine Republican family and having voted against you twice (I wasn't twenty-one until 1939) ... or how much my tardiness related to my own state of being . . . a slow learner. But I did learn about your contributions to American life when I declared my intellectual independence, jokingly told friends that I "went to Harvard and turned Left!" And you'll be pleased perhaps to learn that I finally cast a Democratic vote . . . for Adlai Stevenson, albeit futilely since I'd overreacted to American political ethics in 1948 when traveling Left, way past Harry Truman, to vote for Norman Thomas.

Dear Gardie (grandmother),

When I opened the refrigerator door to fix my lunch a little while ago, I immediately spotted a package of baloney . . . the same one from which I made my lunch yesterday. But somehow today was different; I said to myself, "I'll fry myself a couple of slices in honor of Gardie!" And as I fried it, I said to myself, "I'll close my eyes while I'm eating and conjure up all the images I can of your home on Bartlett Street and what it meant to me." So, that's how I ate my lunch, eyes closed, images flying by . . . your ever-present support and kindness . . . stopping to answer us kids' questions and let us know you were present when we came to see you . . . your constant feeding us baloney . . . with the burned smell frequently permeating nostrils and memory (little did we realize per-haps that that was all that you could afford to feed us cousins as we milled about your table . . .).

And to my Bates College professor, Robert Berkelman, and later a colleague:

Dear Bob,

Somewhere in the dim distant past, when you were serving as my role model for becoming a professor, you remarked that you always responded to communications with some kind of note, postal card, or letter . . . and if you could not respond that you wrote a note saying that you were too busy to respond properly. I liked that paradox. . . . In fact, I adopted that viewpoint as my own, always trying to *connect* with the spirit of a communication, come what, come might . . . also your admonition to do things needing doing and do them immediately so as to do them *only once*! Thank you!

These are only a few of my series of letters to the dead. There are dozens more, including those to Sigmund Freud, Henry David Thoreau, Mark Twain, Loren Eisley, Lord Acton, and many others, both noble and unknown. The most emotional was to Lou Gehrig, who shared many of my father's attributes as hero: enduring, long-suffering, humble of origin. The heart of that letter:

I shall not forget a day in 1936 or 1937 when the rumor went around the factory where I worked that you had died. That was two or three years before you had to "step down" because of your back injury and disease; nor do I have the slightest idea where that rumor originated. It was, however, almost an illustration of synchronicity in light of what happened eventually . . . somehow our tapping into the vibrations of the universe to the effect that you were ill. . . . When you "stepped down," I felt your hot tears run down my face, and I'm not sure that I can finish this letter without continuing to experience their burning. I heard your words on radio; I saw and heard them on a newsreel at the theater; I heard them on Edward R. Murrow's recording, "I Can Hear It Now." I still hear them flowing down the years of our times.

And even today, long after the death of Iron Man Lou and my dad, I sometimes reflect upon the way that writing these letters helped me live through the grief I felt at their deaths. In many ways their memory is a living part of me.

When I read one of these letters to a former student, she suggested that I call the series "Postage Due," since, of course, none of them could ever be delivered. When I once wrote a letter to a man in California who had changed his name to "God," my letter came back from the post office rubber-stamped: "Unable to Deliver: ADDRESS UNKNOWN." This seemed appropriate since humans for millennia have been attempting to locate that address!

Mood Pieces

The subject of holiday newsletters often evokes both anger and joy. Almost a half century ago, after receiving many holiday cards, with no news but only a signature (close to being "Postage Due"), I decided to try to "prime the pump" by sending out what I called "Mood Pieces." These were more than newsy newspieces; rather, I usually sat down to blank paper to convey my current "spirit" or that of our household. I might start with some vague notions about experiences of the year or plans for the following year along with some information that I wished to convey to old friends at holiday time. While we received an occasional complaint (the worst: "You were sexist in not including enough data about Maryllyn"), in general their reception was favorable. While busy in the mid-1960s with evolving programs for Antioch College and the Union Graduate School, I didn't have time to maintain the kind of correspondence that I enjoyed. And this became more critical when I began working with graduate students, one on one, because I felt more of an urge to keep up with their postgraduate lives and gained the impression that my former students/learners felt the same way. So I started "pumping out" Mood Pieces to continue the interaction with those persons. Sometimes I wrote such communications around the edges of an ongoing colloquium. I remember distinctly waking up to a magnificent autumn dawn in Cincinnati, went quickly to my typewriter, looked out the window of the old monastery where we were located, and quickly dashed off a title, "Cinnamon Dawn in Cincinnati." I wrote the mood piece at one sitting and sent it to all learners attending previous colloquia. In fact, I usually entitle these Mood Pieces in a flash, reflecting my mood. Some more recent titles: "To Friends & Roamins Around the Balled-up Park," "A May Day," "Hurrying to Slow Down," "Out Of and In Focus," "Sharp Splinters Off a Log," "My Daily Illusion," "S-W-I-S-S-S-H-H-H," and "Holly Days or Holly Daze?" Long before the Internet became a networking tool, one of my former learners sent accolades in my direction when he wrote a book and tagged me as one of the best "networkers" in the business.

For anybody wishing to emulate this approach to communications I have a few notions. Perhaps the typical newsletter is too contrived, especially if it includes data that's systematized about the family and all of its bewildering offspring; and also, if it's too "goody two-shoes" and excludes material on the downside of daily living. The "mood" approach allows room to be more spontaneous, more "off the cuff." Probably it's no place for pathology, though the pathological person may not realize that she or he is falling into that pit. But, then, there's no reason why writers can't develop multiple lists of recipients, hence suiting a variety of receivers. With the text of computer letters so easy to manipulate, it's easy to eliminate sensitive materials that you're willing to share with some friends but not others. This is not to claim too much for using the Mood Piece as a vehicle to communicating. But it is to encourage such networking. Of course, those using computers can "whomp out" such mood pieces with relative ease. In fact, e-mail may have radically changed the tenor of communicating since its very nature seems to speed up the interaction between users. Possibly it's changed the quality since the exchange of bytes may diminish the amount of reflection that comes occasionally from snail mail. This may be a consequence, but it is not necessarily an inevitability.

Exercise No. 13: Zen and Housekeeping

It's long since time to put housekeeping into the Zen camp since few can agree whether the activity is an art, a science, a commonsense endeavor, or just a plain nuisance. For too many women, especially those who work at a full-time job away from home, "house beautiful" is an impossible dream, a women's magazine nightmare that leads to stress and unrealistic application of the work ethic. In fact, women and their husbands need a housekeeper's bill of rights and wrongs to guide them. This is a first-time effort to provide some of those bills, the unpayable kind! The task here: do some more inventing, using a few guidelines with a major objective, more freedom.

First, a few new perspectives must be achieved whether a house owner or a maid or whoever has the task to do:

- That which is *not* worth doing is not worth doing *well*;

- Assume an attitude that will lessen preparation for visitors; namely, leave at least one dirty corner so that those guests who are looking for dirt will surely find it.

Second, study the U.S. Bill of Rights for clues:

- From Article II on bearing arms: women should insist upon bare arms while doing their work; Dear Abby tells us that some insist upon doing their housework in the nude anyway;

- From Article III on quartering soldiers "without consent of the Owner": since women are family members and homeowners, they should not be suffered to express such consent since they already own their own houses along with the bank, mortgage companies, etc.

- Further inspiration from the bill should be obvious.

Third, re: the cliché about a home being "a man's castle":

- If that's so, let him clean the damn place!

The artistic impulse need not be mystical or mysterious. Most people have it whether they know it or not. As distinguished humanist psychologist Rollo May indicated in a valuable book, they need *The Courage to Create*.[11] Once again, this is to suggest modes of expression that can be fun.

Notes

1. Miranda Seymour, *Robert Graves* (New York: Henry Holt, 1995), pp. 368ff.

2. Roy P. Fairfield, "Transformation," *Pine Island Journal* 1, no. 3 (1999): 7.

3. Roy P. Fairfield, "The Self-Deceiving Prophecy," *Free Inquiry* 6, no. 1 (1985/86): 56–57.

4. Roy P. Fairfield, "Freedom Is Frightening," *Free Inquiry* 1, no. 1 (1980/81): 30–31.

5. Erich Fromm, *Escape from Freedom* (New York: Avon, 1976); Ernest Becker, *Denial of Death* (New York: Free Press, 1985).

6. *Miami Herald*, March 18, 1997, pp. C1–2.

7. Ira Progoff, *At a Journal Workshop* (New York: Dialogue House, 1975).

8. Eugen Herrigel, *Zen in the Art of Archery*, trans. R. F. C. Hull (New York: Pantheon Books, 1953); and Robert M. Pirsig, *Zen and the Art of Motorcycle Maintenance: An Inquiry into Values* (New York: Morrow, 1974).

9. Ralph Barton Perry, *Puritanism and Democracy* (New York: Vanguard, 1944). See chapter 10, "The Moral Athlete," pp. 245–268.

10. David Brazier, *Zen Therapy* (New York: Wiley, 1997).

11. Rollo May, *The Courage to Create* (New York: W. W. Norton, 1975).

CHAPTER 6

The Artistic Impulse

History is full of illustrations or "evidence" of the existence of a wide variety of artistic impulses, ranging from cave-wall drawings to those reflected in modern or contemporary art museum displays. Even graffiti artists would claim such impulses to justify their public paint (and pain?) scapes! Likewise with a vast variety of designs, from those embodied in simple tools to those incorporating complex French curves in their bewildering variety or decorated African huts to glass-walled skyscrapers. The computer revolution and Internet structure are among the most recent illustrations of the creative impulse in action. Archaeological, anthropological, and historical literature is also replete with examples of *how* impulses originated and evolved; these, too, reflect a lengthy continuum ranging from the simple explanation of "necessity is the mother of invention" to application of the idea that role models are the grandmothers and grandfathers of creativity. Note the influences of the ancient Greek, Praxiteles, in sculpture; da Vinci and Michelangelo in engineering, painting, and sculpture; Frank Lloyd Wright in architecture; Mme. Curie and Albert Einstein in science, and so on. This list could be expanded to encyclopedic proportions. Yet, might not a zillion illustrations drive the question back to bedrock, i.e., from whence do artistic impulses come?

Darwin and Creativity Theory

Without the benefit (or perhaps the confusion?) of extensive research into creativity theory, I wish to posit a theory based upon Darwin's biological notions about evolution. It will be recalled that there are three conditions that must be met before evolution may occur; namely,[1]

- there must be a surplus of seeds;

- those who adapt to changing conditions and carry mutations must procreate;

- in the ensuing struggle, the fittest survive as a consequence of "natural selection."

It seems to me that creative impulses, regardless of the cultural contexts in which they appear and grow, require similar conditions. The social context is an equivalence for nature. Surely, it is common knowledge that open societies provide a more favorable climate than closed ones, hence we have the golden ages of ancient Greece or the Italian Renaissance or twentieth-century America.[2] Naturally, too, with more time to perceive the creative impulses and their consequences as measured by ideas, technological feats, or artistic productions, we can literally see what society deems as the fittest that survive. Comparing Russian realism (i.e., "art for Marx's sake," 1918–1989) with a wide variety of artistic expression in the United States and western Europe is another way to measure survival or at least compare communist with democratic creating. Time may be a healer, but it is, paradoxically enough, a destroyer, too. Praxiteles or Michelangelo marbles may survive for only two thousand or even three thousand years by the very nature of its substance. Likewise, the Parthenon or St. Peter's Basilica; yet, one knows that contemporary industrial waste products etch their toxic stains on both. In the same sense the *Mona Lisa*, well preserved over the centuries, will no doubt survive as the fittest better than some of the more transitory metal sculpture which may soon rust away. We know, too, that many of these so-called classics raise questions, the half-life of which becomes centuries, whereas the short-lived and transitory pieces of any art involve questions that are here today and gone tomorrow.

Here is what we *do not* know: What quantity of "seeds" is needed for probable survival (creative impulses and their external products)? We can study the auction prices of Sotheby's, Christie's, or a local auctioneer and use monetary criteria as a way to determine "fittest," or calculate the total nature of the competition from which the high-priced items survived. But there are probably too many variables to use that calculus alone. With great precision we could learn how many patents were applied for, decade by decade since the founding of the American Republic; and it would be just as easy to choose those items that had lasted by virtue of their utility, for instance, the phone, the radio, and the television. But how many ideas for inventions died with the creator or perished for lack of money to apply for a patent? How many were then "reinvented," patented, and survived? In short, the number of seeds, ideas, and creative impulses is obviously larger than we'll ever know. The criteria by which these impulses are judged by those in any particular social context vary considerably. Surely, the nature of the object itself, whether tool or artistic artifact, is something like the half-life of a question; it depends upon the material, who is preserving it, and for what reason. But, as noted, it may "survive" as "fittest" because of utility, supply and demand, artistic expression, value to an individual or institution, or the particular climate at any given moment of time.

With the billions upon billions of creative impulses humans generate and nourish, I would contend that just as biological evolution depends upon mutation and random selection, many such impulses are subject to chance. Equally powerful impulses make their appearance simultaneously in different parts of the world. One survives; another dies. Given the opportunity, we could argue that they are (or were) "equally powerful," pervasive, cogent, beautiful in concept and design and utility. Also, we might argue that the one that died was better than the one that lived; yet, we'd be driven back to Darwinian "rules of evidence" to find the "explanation."

> Aside: A classic example of this issue may be found in the history of anesthesia wherein Crawford Long and William Morton were coinventors of ether; yet, Long did not publish; Morton did; hence Morton's name is the more likely survivor although the competition is documented by story. Oliver Wendell Holmes suggested that this problem could be solved by erecting a simple monument: "To Ether!"

Art as a Survival Imperative

A corollary and/or the "engine" that drives the Darwinian *process* might be expressed in the concept of "survival imperative." Just as a species does not survive if it doesn't produce many seeds, subject to environmental pressures, the temporary existence of human beings is a powerful factor. Viewed from another angle of vision, one may easily inquire: What if humans had no memory yet lived forever? How strong would the creative impulse be? Or assume that humans lived forever and retained memory of varying qualities and quantities? What implications might these changed conditions pose for the creative impulse? for education? or for family legacies?

We know, for instance, that humans are conscious of procreativity as the major route to human longevity, both as a species and a social organism. Just as species have died out, so have families that failed to procreate. But has their legacy vanished? There is an old expression, "Life is short and art is long." In a nutshell this is an objective fact with overwhelming empirical evidence to support its truth and surely a factor in longevity. While an average person (however defined) may not develop a complex theory from this simple fact, nevertheless, the road to "eternity"/survival is cluttered with the skeletons of persons who attempted to invent the better mousetrap, build a new kind of organization, paint in a mode never seen before, and so on. While most humans will admit that they "can't take it with them," this does not preclude their effort to perpetuate their heritage in both traditional and unique ways. Some invent new philanthropic foundations and institutions for enhancing social good; others leave substantial numbers of paintings and/or unique collections to museums or libraries. On the American landscape we have so many "halls of fame," more "collectible" groups, and so on, that it is theoretically possible that in five more centuries the landscape will be completely paved by these monuments to legacy. And among them some are symbolized by "halls of shame"! And probably that's okay. Better that a person design and whittle a new toothpick than become the familiar couch potato! Better that she "consume" a bushel of acrylic paints than a bushel of fast food eaten on the run. And in the same vein, better that she design a new graffiti than gossip her neighbor to death over the back fence where she's practicing that new design.

> Aside: Those having read John Steinbeck's *Travels with Charley* will recall his suggestion about assuring the family's heritage by assembling piles of "junk," mothballing it much as the navy saves vessels to "fight another day." Then in the Steinbeck scenario, when the junk is cleaned up in another generation or two, what now seems like junk will probably include precious relics from the past! Another avenue to survival.[3]

In short, since "life is short and art is long," let each person attempt to express himself, regardless of the product, as a way to establish a claim on his own heritage or legacy. It is my private opinion that thousands of women in the United States could have gained a unique kind of immortality if only they had stitched their initials or names on the millions of embroideries, quilts, and other so-called crafts that they made for centuries. This does not denigrate the *process* through which they extended their own being from one generation to the next, by creating enduring artifacts. Regrettably, we know all too little about some of those stitching persons although we have a good sense of their contribution to America's enduring heritage, however anonymous. One can only hope that those currently extending this heritage will capture another dimension of the creative process; namely, what this does to the creators' self-concepts. Still another avenue to survival.

It is my bias that it does not matter so much *what* the creative impulse is or *what* it produces as it does *that* individuals follow their inclination to create. While we might argue that the impetus to create "fine art" assumes a "higher" (more complex) plane than crafts, social, economic, and political forces will "regulate" those differences the survival of the fittest "rules" and/or "laws" take over. I would contend that every human being, except for the very ill, has the potential to manifest some kind of creative impulse and should be encouraged to do so. It has been painful during the past decade to watch the attack on the arts, whether it's the local school board cutting art teachers from its budget or the National Endowment for the Humanities experiencing severe downsizing. It was encouraging to read journalist Vartan Gregorian's view about steps to improve the public schools in the popular Sunday supplement *Parade*, and learn that one of the ten steps he recommends is to "Restore the arts as a major element in education." He goes on to say that "We've made a tremendous mistake in diminishing or eliminating art, music, and dance as fluff or frills. . . . It's almost impossible to overemphasize the significance of the creative arts in education."4

But, again, the impulse to create, to extend human insights from one generation to the next, to strengthen a legacy, needs reinforcement of process, regardless of product. When the impulse translates into process, how does that enhance the quality of life? How can we capture that enhancement via poetry, knitted garments, new music and dance compositions, carpentry projects, murals on bathroom walls; again, it's the *that* and *not* (necessarily) the *what*. And both are possible. By discussing journal keeping as well as the nature of some of the processes in other parts of this volume, including the one that follows, I hope that there may be meaning in the notion of creative projects as related to survival.

Haiku and You

The haiku, a Japanese form of poetry and insight, is eminently capable of reflecting vast varieties of creative impulses. There is an important literature on its history and centrality in Japanese life. Millions of Japanese people enter the process, and even the emperor writes his annual stint of haiku poems that become public. And while there are skeptics who say that haiku cannot be written in English, I believe that anybody can write them in any language. Those wishing to explore the topic will find ample material in Bruce Ross's *Haiku Moment: An Anthology of Contemporary North American Haiku*; or consult the bibliography of the present volume and/or endnote number 7 of this chapter.[5]

I refer you to my Do-It-Yourself Haiku-Writing Kit in Exercise No. 10, below, and recommend that regardless of your educational or writing background, pick up pen or pencil, then take your five senses outdoors, preferably into a quiet patch of nature where you can take a deep breath and let your senses go.

In general, children adapt quickly to the conditions that breed haiku because they're not "hung up" on language syntax. Let's look at a couple of Vermont seventh-graders writing, some years ago:

> Come flower, pop up
> and see the bright and good world,
> don't be afraid, come.

> Kitten in the snow
> wondering what the flakes are
> that makes him so cold.

Or a more recent one by a twelve-year-old with whom I exchange haiku:

> If it takes a town
> to raise only one child
> who watches the sheep?[6]

The major objective is to capture a moment, motion, or emotion in a precise piece of space, time, and psyche (or preferably space-time-psyche). But let me return to the basic elements: the *American Heritage Dictionary* defines haiku as "a Japanese lyric poem of a fixed seventeen-syllable form that often simply points to a thing or a pairing of things in nature that has moved the poet." The seventeen syllables, in the classical form, assume shape in three lines of five, seven, and five syllables each; usually they refer or infer a season of the year. There is no demanding rhythm or rhyme unless you want to include them. The best classical type will frequently take a quick turn at the end of the second line, suggesting perhaps a life or death theme or observation. An early one of my own:

> We weave webs of trust
> in tall trees of apple green,
> beyond a scythe's reach.

They may include a dash of whim, as for instance, one I wrote in a bird sanctuary:

> Cardinal whistles
> wolf-like across hibiscus,
> his joy's for the birds.

No question, writing them for more than three decades has sharpened my powers of observation, and the ability to see the nuances of color, hear the sounds of nature more keenly, and feel the poignancy of life-death issues. One also comes to appreciate the potentiality for the use of words as well as the value of their ambiguity. If you dabble in acrylics or are keen on photography, writing haiku will shape and sharpen your creative impulses.

Metaphors and images will pop up everywhere. Whereas it's awkward to carry a camera into some social and physical settings, there's little problem carrying a pad of paper, writing implements, or scraps of paper on which to scribble.

From a jet at 30,000 feet:

> Roads crawl like spider
> webs across rolling woodscapes
> snaring eyes that fly.

In a supermarket:

> Olives row on row
> for dozens of glassy feet,
> martinis complete.

While walking through an old house:

> Termites shave timbers
> piling sawdust for winter,
> will house crash today?

And by the sea:

> Hissing waves sound . . .
> singing, crashing, siblings all,
> slyly in July.

> Lobster boats plying
> rocky coastal coves, making
> all landlubbers drool!

But most importantly the haiku form describes images wherein anybody can feel that powerful impulse to capture an experience in word pictures much as one can do it with photos. So more importantly than reading mine, why not create your own? Experience your own sharpened perception, your own joy of putting high compression upon an impression. There's nothing secret or sacred about the process; nor need one be a crystal-ball gazer even as she becomes a better see-er!

Exercise No. 14: Doing Haiku

Go to a beach or zoo or park or isolated countryside; go with a trusted friend, one not inclined to be judgmental. Discuss the nature of haiku and what you know about this poetic form and/or one or two that you've written. "Prime the pump" by alternating descriptions of some of the things that you are seeing, smelling, tasting, touching . . . use all your senses.

Then, in due time (don't rush it!), volunteer or have your friend volunteer what may become the first line of a haiku:

—— —— —— —— ——

Simply find a five-syllable phrase to fill the blanks.
Then, you or your partner take a turn to propose a middle line:

—— —— —— —— —— —— ——,

a seven-syllable impression or expression.

Finally, still taking turns, have the second person find the five-syllable completion of the haiku.

—— —— —— —— ——

Don't worry if it's not "perfect." Also don't worry if you do *not* have the "correct" number of syllables, or if it does *not* say anything about life or death and the seasons, or even fails to take a sharp turn at the end of the second line. You can always polish or even throw the words out. In short, don't be too hard on yourselves. The haiku requires honest interaction with the natural world; keep the interaction impressionistic, *avoid* intellectualizing it. Also, *avoid* abstract notions; keep to a close and direct interaction with that external world. After you and your partner have shared your perceptions of colors, fragrances, subtle tastes, and sharp surfaces (either in imagination or reality), in short after you've had the *fun* of experiencing the creative impulses either in a single day or many, then you might wish to become more playful. Remind one another that it could be dangerous to see the entire world through a seventeen-syllable grid; and, keeping the spirit of haiku writing, simply jot down descriptions of whatever you see, regardless of the number of syllables you use. This is a point at which you might wish to consult Ross's book mentioned above, or other books in the same genre.[7]

Above all, keep a "light" mood, receptive to any and all impressions and open to filtering them through your senses, including intuition. After writing a few hundred or thousand, you'll be glad you did and wish you'd begun to test your creative impulses years before!

Grooks Anonymous: Dogged and Dog-Legged Doggerel

Webster's speaks of English doggerel as "low in style and irregular in measure; undignified; trivial . . . esp. burlesque or comic." Although its origins may be "unknown," doggerel is probably as old as folksinging; after all, that's a source of joy, ritual, and so-called low comedy. And most of us have written doggerel whether we've known it or not. After all, birthday and Valentine's Day "poetry" is full of such stanzas as "Roses are red/violets are blue/sugar is sweet/and so are you."

But a generation ago Piet Hein, a Danish engineer, brought forth a somewhat new design of doggerel. They were more cryptic, had sharper endings. He called his creations "grooks," and wrote a series of such books, illustrating them in a deliciously provocative, humorous, and enticing manner.[8] They had every manner of line-ending rhymes. His new twist was to add the graphics as well as effect a critical bite into his observations, one that makes the reader do a double take upon completing his verse. And whether Hein is commenting upon our precarious coexistence with the threat of nuclear extinction or the esoteric nature of modern poetry, one cannot finish reading a grook without being jolted into thoughtful consideration of some human dilemma. As with haiku, grooks are both easy and fun to write. But whereas the haiku seems to flourish in natural settings, grooks grow best in tight emotional, political, or social situations. Since I began writing them more than a quarter century ago, I've written no fewer than ten thousand during seminars; waiting in line for bank tellers or postal clerks to say "the next person, please"; at weddings, funerals, and graduations. Wherever I've been on a loose pulley or working at the multiple levels of awareness discussed in chapter 5, my critical faculties have bubbled over with grooks. While recently in an accountant's office, waiting and watching him finish my state income tax when I had no relevant input, I scribbled eight with barely a thought. My first followed a question triggered by the monitor on his computer, "Do you still regard the figures on your machine as something like magic?" As he looked up to say, "Yes!" and continued with the tax forms, I scribbled:

> A magical eye
> computerized tax
> designed for when
> some folks are lax . . .

This led to:

> Make out your tax
> write out full salary
> send all to IRS
> don't linger or dally.

In short, I dialogued with myself while immersing myself in the busyness of tending to a detail that filled the chinks of time during the annual tax ritual. Since I dislike waiting without doing something constructive, writing grooks becomes a fulfillment of the creative urge.

More recently at the Miami zoo, I stopped at several exhibits to focus on animal characteristics, much as Ogden Nash did when writing poems about animal peculiarities.

> Think of a giraffe
> thirsty for water
> stretching her neck
> higher than she oughta . . .

> View six kangaroos
> with newborns in pocket
> and even the next
> genes in the docket . . .

While not as humorous as Nash's famous doggerel about animals, that matters not. Simply write what you feel the animal might feel. Or try a haiku as an entree to grooks:

> Life's like a Bach fugue
> voices coming and going
> in each new season

Isn't it true that once a fugue is in process, with each voice introducing and repeating a composer's theme in an orderly pattern, that awareness of the absent voices is a vital part of the total assemblage of voices? Perhaps that's a major function of silences between notes in any piece of music, intrinsic to establishing rhythms.

In some way that phenomenon is a vital factor in my behavior at most meetings, whether they are seminars involving several persons, a class of one hundred, a condo board meeting, or a dialogue with another person. Each meeting usually has a main theme, major and minor threads of discussion, the dominant voices, and the subordinate. Over the past several decades I have filled a two-foot stack of yellow legal pads with notes or minutes of the externals of those meetings. Most of my "doodling" has taken the form of writing grooks. I've faithfully "recorded" the "minutes" or dominant points down the left-hand side of my yellow pads (sometimes even converting them to the "official" minutes), the grooks (also haiku and free verse) down the right sides of the pages. Many of my associates who have seen me do this or with whom I've shared my processes suggest that there is symbolism in the right and left locations, symbolism related to right and left brain functions. Whether true or not, I cannot say for sure.

What remains interesting to me is the fact that I can usually reread a page from a meeting that I attended ten to twenty years ago and reconstruct the session at many levels. There is always the main argument or theme, much as one might take notes at a college lecture or write minutes from a formal meeting; but, perhaps more importantly, the grooks capture the emotional tones and/or images and/or gestalts which I sensed at the time of the meeting. The two columns of writing complement one another; and, while they may not have the clarity or impact of a video or tape recording, they are like the several voices of the Bach fugue, the net result of which recapitulate the several dimensions of a "moment" of human experience.

To me the grook has been an important tool for such situations. I only regret that I did not learn to draw well enough to effect the impact that Piet Hein makes in his grooks books. Using them as I do, however, not only leaves me with a written record reflecting various levels of creative consciousness, but it also serves another very important function: doing it enables me to maintain my "sanity" during terribly dull, "insane," and/or routine meetings; when the air becomes overheated, this process-writing enables me to ride through the electrical climate without blowing my own emotional fuses. At one level I hear and process the "video" account of the controversy; at another level I sketch my own emotional climate with words—a kinetic explosion.

During an intense decade of serving on many doctoral committees, I sometimes reviewed with "candidates" the notes from the left side of my yellow pages as well as the grooks from the right. Also, at appropriate times I typed the grooks or free verse for the benefit of "my" learners, usually requesting that they be kept confidential. After all, other members of a given committee didn't always need or necessarily welcome my reactions. Sometimes my observations were not very complimentary when other committee members stood in the way of conflict resolution and/or failed to function as learning facilitators. Learners in question understood that and furthered their own quest for a degree by soft-pedaling such conflict. My poems, they claimed, added dimensions they couldn't see, hear, or feel.

Clerihews

Recently, I had the good fortune to be introduced to another poetic form which is becoming much fun. It seems that one Edmund Clerihew Bentley played around with a unique kind of verse in his journal, and his friend G. K. Chesterton illustrated what came to be known as "clerihews."[9] At first it was all a sort of joke, involving odd sketches about some of the world's most famous people, for instance, Sir Christopher Wren, Teddy Roosevelt, and a few Roman emperors. One may infer structure by reading a few. About Bentley's clerihew, "Frederick the Great," which runs:

> Frederick the Great
> Became King at twenty eight.
> In a fit of amnesia
> He invaded Silesia.

Bentley remarks, "one must not . . . confine oneself to what is historic, in the large sense, about the life that is in question. One has to depict the man as he was, not his achievement only."[10] My friend and colleague, Roy Couch, a fellow Mainer who introduced me to the form, delights in playing with words and gave me permission to quote the following:

The Kennedy clan
Has lost another man
A tragic circumstance,
in life's macabre dance.

Astronaut Neil Armstrong
Said that 30 years isn't that long
Since he walked on the moon;
but he won't go back soon.

In short, the rhyme scheme is a, a, b, b.

With my experience and joy in writing grooks and limericks, I found it a fairly easy rhyme scheme to follow. Also, it's okay to be "naughty" though there's not as much room or tradition for making scatological observations as in writing limericks. And, of course, public figures are sitting targets for quick stabs at their personas. When, for instance, Hillary Clinton, still First Lady in the White House, considered running for the Senate, how natural to make the observation that

I fear that Hillary
will go to the pillory
not as a witch
but lacking a stitch . . .

Russians and NATO
exchanging a HO HO
just who's got power
to control the hour?

In short, it's another form to test your sensitivity, adaptability, and sense of humor to laugh at both the world and yourself.

Attack the news
with Clerihews
lighten with jokes
thrust with pokes . . .

New Uses for the Muse

In addition to the above use of grooks to facilitate learning, both mine and "my" learners', I've used poetry in another context that has implications for teacher training. John Holt's *How Children Fail* led me to poetry as a means of rationalizing time and moment-to-moment reflection of classroom reality.[11] He suggests that observers should watch students, not the teacher, if they want to "see it as it is." I was doing just that in an upstate Vermont classroom when "my" student Dale remarked rather casually, "In the days before we were so affluent . . . ." Just as Dale uttered that generalization, I spied a rather shabby fellow sitting near the window of the classroom. Something moved behind him, and my line of vision shifted to laundry hanging dejectedly from a clothesline on a nearby porch. The house was a slum by any standard, and I suddenly wondered, "How many of Dale's pupils live in that house? Does Dale know?"

I began to scribble in the margins of notes that I was making about Dale's teaching. When the bell rang and the students left the classroom, I invited him to join me at the back of the room. I pointed to the slum and asked him the questions that I'd just asked myself. He said he didn't know who lived there. Whereupon I shared with him my scribbled lines:

Do students
see the flats
and squalor
thru panes
so dirty
they screen
the rotten sides
the tattered
clotheslines and
and cluttered porches?
Can poverty
in textbooks match
the broken windows
shoddy styles
unpainted walls
a
landscape
to
pierce
the eyeballs?

During the next two classes that day, I pursued the same course as I watched "my" student teachers interact with their learners. I became more convinced that this approach might complement the work of the eminent social scientist J. P. Flanders, who designed a method of sociogram (or weighted lines of relationships among students and teachers in a classroom) to determine the significance of their interaction. This he believed would reflect the classroom as a dynamic cauldron of learning, not simply where teachers served as peripatetic encyclopedias simply "dishing it out" didactically.

The next day was equally insightful as I stood in a school corridor waiting to enter a classroom. Again I scribbled "madly" and even while writing I was aware that it would require a James Joyce writing *Ulysses* or another *Odyssey* by Niko Kazantzakis to do justice to the billions of interactions in that hallway in those few minutes in that school. Also it contrasted sharply with the experience I'd had farther upstate. The subsequent session was rather dull, substantively. Julie was "uptight" about my presence although we were not using grades in the training program. Her body was somewhat rigid, and she was relying upon that old teacher's crutch, calling on those she knew had the answers; meanwhile, one whole cornerful of boys were "out of it." I knew that she cared; and despite the gray, winter weather outside and the rather warm psychological climate inside, she carried on. After class, I shared my perceptions:

> Does the whir
> of the fan
> drown brain
> stirrings
> amid smog—
> and words
> of ninth-graders
> . . . or blackboard
> scratchings
> etch
> knowledge
> and character
> on pliable cells
> near bright maps?
> Ought answers
> chanced
> crush

inertia
of the mindless
and minding
while kids
sense
caring?

Our conversation after class was both pleasant and honest. Somehow the poetry, however perceived, closed emotional and authority gaps which may have existed. It was certainly more valuable than any number of mathematical sociograms which I could have shared with her.

Thus evolved a process which I've used over the years. Despite various barriers, I became deeply involved with white teachers in essentially black, inner-city schools, white and black teachers working as Peace Corps volunteers in West Africa, and young and middle-aged instructors in a variety of college settings. Although faculty in our teacher-training program opted to use video for capturing student teachers and interns in very difficult urban contexts, I continued to use the grook and free-verse poetry approach as a major means of "seeing" and facilitating their growth. This is not to argue that poetry is *the* medium or panacea for solving the variety of problems new teachers have as they attempt to become acclimated. Rather, if insight and learning result from changing one's angle of vision, from gaining new awareness of one's functioning in any given setting, from recognizing the ambiguities and pregnancies of one's own educational matrices, then perhaps the metaphor, the rhyme, the play on words—even the occasional pun—may complement the videotape, the audiotape, and the several forms of sociogram.

In a sense, too, any prospective author may well capture in words what is almost impossible in video or photo *if* she wishes to be a voyeur. For instance, as I rushed around the state of Vermont visiting classes, I was struck by the incongruity of the length of skirts "girls" wore during the cruel winters. So I wrote a limerick:

Half Past Fahrenheit

If miniskirts get minnier
and lasses' legs get skinnier,
those bony knees
will surely freeze
and higher exposures sinnier . . .

Since I've written thousands of such grooks and free verse during the past four decades, it's virtually impossible to provide samples that fit every situation; but, the "uses" which I discuss here may suggest a utility that could be enabling in any number of social, economic, political, and psychological contexts. For instance, in family contexts, corporate training programs, political caucuses, and individual and group counseling.

Red Coals, Black Ivy

Despite the shameful history of teacher compensation in this century (and every other century!), few will deny the immensity of teacher influence in human life in every century! And while teachers may earn kudos for their impact upon learners of every age, we still know all too little about the pros and cons of that impact. For instance, what if we had documentation of the following nature:

- How much learning results from pure suggestion? from didactics?

- Samples of student "diaries" from a single elementary teacher's classes for a whole year? *Plus* the answers to activity during "my summer vacation" or materials from several years' collections?

- Excerpts from a teacher's diary for those same years?

- A video record of a middle school's classes for a year? also high school? adult diaries and/or autobiographies of a few of those learners ten years later that would include their reflections upon teacher impact?

With such materials we could learn more about mental and physical development. What about the quality of evidence to support well-known anthropologist Ashley Montagu, who contends that life both in and out of the womb is of a continuous skein; in short, rather than "growing old" humans "grow young." Or to paraphrase Wordsworth's famous insight, that the child is father of the parent, physiologically, psychologically, intellectually.

If one accepts the evidence that Montagu presents in his insightful *Growing Young*,[13] then any activity that threatens to inhibit or destroy human development whether that activity is conscious or unconscious, kills a part of the person. And we do not know all that is to be known about the power of suggestion. When I have been commended as a teacher for some of my so-called successes in promoting human growth, I sometimes, with histrionic and whimsical flare, respond, "Of course, I don't know how many persons I've killed." When that comment produces raised eyebrows, I've asked, "Can we know how many forms of killing there are in classrooms or in general on a college campus?" I learned this the hard way during my first years of teaching at Bates College. I wrote about the experience in a manuscript that "never saw the light of day" although I shared it with colleagues long after the dramatic events. It involved a fellow named Jim:

He was a junior, literally tall, dark, and handsome. Sitting in the front row, he laughed at my jokes, took part in discussions, gave me feedback which every young teacher needs to reinforce confidence. He was a key member of the theater group, and we loved to watch him wrap himself into a part so thoroughly it was difficult to tell which was body and which garment. In short, he was part of that beautiful human landscape so much more important than ivy and architecture on any campus. Then one morning at 5:20 I had a horrifying dream, so traumatizing it woke me up. I was helping an undertaker friend put Jim in a casket when he suddenly sat bolt upright and exclaimed, "You can't *do* this to me!" His remark *was characteristic*. I couldn't go back to sleep. I woke my wife to relate the dream. Later that morning as we entered an auditorium-classroom, I, the amateur psychologist, said, "Hey, Jim, have I ever shown you any hostility?" He said, "No, why?" Then I told him about the dream. He laughed heartily, patted me on the shoulder, and we strolled into the room together. That was on a Tuesday. The following Saturday night, during the half-time pause at a basketball game, I thought I saw strange things happening. From the gym balcony I observed the athletic director running about like the proverbial headless chicken. He summoned the president; then, the school doctor left. What was happening? Like the dream itself, I momentarily forgot the strange events during the game's second-half excitement . . . until I reached home and the phone rang. It was a colleague asking, "Have you heard? Jim was killed by an automobile skidding into him and his girlfriend down on College Street?" My knees buckled! Had I contributed to his death? Was I as guilty as the driver? How could I ever know?

I made careful notes, talked with my psychologist-colleague, even phoned the president to assuage my conscience, mulled over the total gestalt. I then began collecting evidence of incidents where my own interaction with my students might be perceived as growthful or destructive. I conceived a manuscript in which my biographical sketch of the learner ran down the left-hand page; and, facing it was my free verse in the same vogue as Edgar Lee Masters' poems, spoken by the occupants of the Spoon River cemetery. The Jim story was first; hence, facing the above account of Jim's life and death, I wrote his speech:

> I cannot speak harshly
> about so grave
> a matter as death
> which cut me off
> even as I grew
> in joy and sorrow
> but I could wish
> to rest his fears
> for having stumbled
> in a dream across
> hints of my early demise.
> Jan and I took destiny
> into our own hands
> by walking down the icy street

> that fateful winter night
> it was as simple as that.

The verse continues for another couple dozen lines. Obviously, I was writing through my own grief and concerns. But the "story" continued for another ninety pages as I dialogued with myself and some of my students about their deaths in college learning situations which should have promoted life! More paradoxes and ironies! More incidents of interaction with students and colleagues who tried to take their lives or who nearly self-destructed via alcohol and drugs, who were unconscious of behavior which nearly killed others. The manuscript rests in my archives under several titles, including *Shadows on the Walls* and *Black Ivy on Red Bricks*. It was my effort to raise consciousness about both living and deadly moments where it's assumed learning is always positive.

The Poem-Letter

The poem-letter is a spontaneous happening. It can, of course, assume any form, *from* sonnet *to* doggerel *to* traditional verse of any kind, even a single haiku, sent as a letter. I have used all of these modes to communicate with students, friends, family, and colleagues; they may be less useful for formal communications regarding a position, legal situation, or other matter where playfulness and the free use of metaphor might neither be understood nor appreciated.

I've found the poem-letter to be most useful in reconnecting with a long-lost associate or in sending a note of congratulations upon the occasion of an engagement, wedding, or birth. Or even in sending a note of condolence where a card or similar communication seems stale or doesn't fit. The beauty of this mode of communication is that you can be as creative as you dare. While formal verse is often difficult to write in emotional situations, free verse enables a maximum amount of freedom both in definition and acceptance by the reader.

I find it most useful when sitting down to a blank piece of paper or computer screen to "reach out" and "seize a metaphor" by an adjective or image associated with the person to whom I'm writing. For instance, I have a former student-friend whose first name is Ulysses. Hence, when I start to write him, I simply say

Dear Ulysses . . .

O ye of the Great Journey . . .

then I usually "pick it up there" to expand upon his journey, my own, or our joint travel, eventually creating a verse that flows through both our experiences.

Another first line or two that I've used occasionally, especially for birthdays, anniversaries, and similar situations, is:

When in the course of human events
the days grow long and situations tense

Similarly:

There are milestones
smiling tones

Create your own form: ?????? ------------------ _____
or .... ?????

Consistent with the appropriate emotion, I usually write a poem-letter in one sitting and keep it to a single page, even if I have to use double or triple spacing to make the fit. I say whatever comes through my head and fingers; I do not worry about rhyme or rhythm; if it occurs, fine; if not, that's okay, too. And I don't strive for any other traditional effect, such as alliteration, internal rhymes, and/or niceties. If they happen, fine. If humor is appropriate, I include it. If an apt quote comes to mind, I cite it even if I have to look up the exact words at a later moment. One that occurs to me at this moment is Maurice Maeterlinck's observation in the *Bluebird* where the Belgian playwright says that those living on in our hearts and minds never die. It's not that I have a large repertoire of exact quotes in mind, but like most persons I can dip a few from memory's wellsprings as well as a well-worn copy of Bartlett's *Familiar Quotations.* But it's important to put the flow of words over striving for precision or as Wordsworth suggested, let "a spontaneous overflow of powerful feelings" govern the tone of the letter. I do not hesitate to use words from folk songs or references from music, painting, or history. Again, a poem-letter is not a demonstration of scholarship; rather it's an expression of feeling. But the writer should feel *free* to use whatever occurs at the moment, very existentially.

I do have what has become a conventional conclusion for birthday letters, not only wishing friends a "Happy Birthday," but also that every day may be a "Happy Mirthday." I see no harm in leaving the recipient of any poem-letter with a smile.

Let me include a Golden Anniversary sample, for critiquing if you wish:

Dear P—— & D——

There are milestones
& stony miles
smiles revisited
on the paths to tomorrow

so (no borrowing from Hallmark):
we send GOLDEN THOUGHTS
to cancel
all the "oughts"
of things we should have done
like jump into a jet
and bet with you at the Count of Fifty

('twoulda been
kinda nifty!)

but we know that your children
will gather round
and make the ground sacred
where you walk
and you'll soon be here in Maine
where we can talk.
HAPPY ANNIVERSARY
        &
               Love,

Or one upon the occasion of a family death:

Dear Lin,

To learn that your dad
had joined the Great Caravan
evoked mem'ries
of Baker's woods
of shoulds & don'ts
around the Old Shop
the smell of batteries
(auto arteries)

& your father's tensest gaze
but kindly mien

(with Clarence's
     somewhere
               in-between)

of MY dad's high regard
for your dad's person & skill
knowing that whatever the problem
there was a will
to solve it with aplomb
not just stand around dumb and let it go away . . .

We send good thoughts
for his constructive life
and know somewhere in the Cosmos
he's cutting through problems
               with his laser-brain knife . . .

The best way to shape the beauty and utility of this form is simply to put on your imagination cap and *write!* And to launch most artistic effort, that usually takes risking and courage!

Spontaneity and Being

Whether Shakespeare foreshadows the stereotype of the artistic temperament or merely echoes it, I don't know. Certainly Western society has both honored and ridiculed the artist over the past four centuries since the Bard wrote, in *Midsummer Night's Dream*,

The lunatic, the lover, and the poet
Are of imagination all compact . . .
The poet's eye, in a fine frenzy rolling,
Doth glance from heaven to earth, from
    earth to heaven;
And as imagination bodies forth
The forms of things unknown, the poet's pen
Turns them to shapes, and gives to airy nothing
A local habitation and a name . . .[14]

This is consistent with the stereotype of the artist (including the poet, at least as a metaphor) as being temperamental, willing to starve, replete with observations and expressions that are off the chart or curves of "normality," less worthy of societal support, bizarre, emotionally unbalanced, ugly, and so on. And yet an anonymous quatrain reflects the other side of the coin:

Artists strive
while alive
and get ahead
when they're dead . . .

So very frequently, an artist's perceptions are so far ahead of her time that the times do not catch up for decades or centuries. In fact, some social historians and philosophers argue that that is one of the functions of the artist.[15] Jane Austen's novels are only now being fully appreciated; Pablo Picasso begins to look "old hat" in light of contemporary graphic technology; Vincent van Gogh's ear-severing episode is now occasionally emulated to convey a message; and Frank Lloyd Wright, so far ahead of his day in architectural design, is now perceived almost as a classicist. Frequently, too, these judgments are an inevitable consequence of supply and demand. When death claims an artist, the flow of words, notes, or colored strokes, her creative impulses cease. Hence Sotheby's or Christie's can bid these scarcest of artifacts into the sky even though the creator died before her time had arrived.

Another paradoxical subtheme of artistic temperament is: If the "academy" accepts an artist, be that "academy" the Nobel or Pulitzer committees, an institution such as the royal academy of whatever, or if a university incorporates an artist into its faculty and curriculum, then it is highly probable that the artist's creative days are waning. And if so-called professionals seize upon the artist and "professionalizes" her, whether that seizure is in the form of a prize or an institutional norm, the mediocritization has probably begun. Perhaps it all relates to criteria by which the novelist, poet, playright, architect, composer, dancer, and others are judged. Such terms as "excellent" and "brilliant" have been used so often, especially by the mass media, that they seem to have lost their utility. Naturally, the truly spontaneous person is suspicious of critics; judgment and the threat thereof surely kill the creative impulse. As Saul Bass dramatically states in his film, *Why Man Creates*, there is nothing like judgment or the threat of it, to destroy the creative impulse.[16] Perhaps it is heart versus head at its most protean and stereotypical juncture? The mass media's gluttony for material is another killer of the creative impulse; if artists are busy forcing that impulse, mediocrity seems almost inevitable even though billions of such impulses are cascading into the Darwinian flow of events.

Aside: A query or two: to what extent does Edgar Allan Poe serve as a prototype for the impact of alcohol upon artists, or Allan Ginsburg a prototype for the drug-user?

This is *not* to suggest that all artists are created equal or should be judged accordingly. It *is* to suggest, paradoxically, that once spontaneity if programmed, wherein is it spontaneous? Also, what does it do to the artist's sense of being? And is it any wonder that it is only logical that scientists claim one language while poets identify with another? Indeed, there is such a plethora of creative impulses today it is "no wonder" that it may require a century to sort it all out. Meanwhile, such a time lag may be the soil in which those who focus on collectibles may plant their money and reputations for being "shrewd." However spontaneous such collecting may be, that artistry acquires a distinctly different shape, reminding us of an earlier reference to John Steinbeck's recommendation in *Travels with Charley*.

The "lover and madman" syndrome which Shakespeare presents may be recollected in the biographies of Robert Graves, surely one of the greatest romantic poets of the twentieth century. His constant search for and consorting with female muses surely affected what might be considered a rational/normal living style. Yet, would he have produced such an enormous volume of poetry and other writing if he hadn't had his muses? And while he may have been "off the scale" by most norms, who would have wanted to declare him a "madman" and committed to an "asylum"? One could argue, of course, that he created his own private asylum. In my judgment his life is a prime "case" for the study and rewarding of spontaneity and being, a life which might inspire some modern Homer or Shakespeare to place him in the flow of the human journey—an odyssey such as that of Joyce or Kazantzakis. Wouldn't any writer aspire to join the flow, the odyssey?

Sense Deprivation and Enhancement

We identify the artist as a person with enhanced sensitivities and, frequently, sensibilities: senses keenly honed to listen to a muse, sharpen discipline, tune into the universe of language, sounds, colors, lines, motions, and emotions. Michael Gelb, in *How to Think Like Leonardo Da Vinci*, spells out the nature of those sensitivities and sensibilities, and even suggests "Seven Steps to Genius Every Day."[17] And yet, much has been written about the blindness of Homer, Oedipus, and John Milton; the deafness of Ludwig van Beethoven; the multiple-sensory deprivation of Helen Keller. In fact, such instances are used as evidence that one can do what he sets his mind to, the overcoming of handicaps, the triumphs and tragedies of confronting the universe in all of its benign and perverse forms. A 1995 film titled *Mr. Holland's Opus* incorporated a powerful subtheme when the musician-teacher experienced the birth of a deaf son. And just as Beethoven "heard" his music through vibrations he obtained by lying on the floor, so did the young son appreciate music by sitting on the amplifier. We speak of persons, even musicians who are "tone deaf" and artists who are color blind.

Such illustrations may easily be used as role models for the handicapped and not perceived as mere human jetsam and flotsam where the creative impulse is absent. At their rawest extreme such examples could be crippling to the human spirit as well as the creative. But since most people have some kind of deprivation, of physical health, mental shortcoming, or social and political blindness, there may not be any such person as "average." If each person could perceive herself as part of the total diversity of humanity, then it might be easier to promote tolerance of one another. Rather than bathing in self-pity, each person might strive to overcome the shortcomings of self as well as those of others and let the creative impulse burst, wherever, whenever, however!

One experiences a giant leap forward upon becoming aware of and accepting the fact that individuals, communities, religions, races, genders, and nations perceive the world from many (and sometimes different) angles of vision. Indeed, one cannot walk in another's shoes, sandals, or stilts without "trying them on for size." If people were not so judgmental about others' appearances, behaviors, and beliefs without really trying to understand what they project as seeing, we might have fewer wars, local feuds, and angry confrontations. My next chapter encourages new seeing and being.

Notes

1. Sir William Dampier, *A History of Science and Its Relations with Philosophy and Religion* (Cambridge, Eng.: University Press, 1949), pp. 276–77.

2. See Lester Thurlow, "Building Wealth," *Atlantic Monthly* 283, no. 6 (1999): 57–69.

3. John Steinbeck, *Travels With Charley* (New York: Bantam, 1963).

4. Vartan Gregorian, *Parade* (March 23, 1997).

5. Bruce Ross, *Haiku Moment* (Boston: Charles Tuttle, 1993).

6. With permission of Emily and Diane Lynch, August 7, 1999. We often exchange haiku.

7. Try reading aloud from the brief prefaces of the Peter Pauper Press books such as *Cherry Blossoms* (1960) or *Japanese Haiku* (1955/56). For historical perspective you might try Robert Hass, ed., *The Essential Haiku: Versions of Basho, Buson and Issa* (Hopewell, N.J.: Ecco Press, 1994). Or a fun book, Stephen Addis, ed., *A Haiku Menagerie: Living Creatures in Poems and Prints* (New York: Weatherhill, 1994). If you're interested in integrating artistic photography and haiku, see Ann Atwood's splendid *The Mood of Earth* (New York: Scribner, 1971).

8. Cambridge, Mass.: MIT Press, 1966. Others were published by Doubleday, 1969, 1970, 1973; Basil Blackwood, 1972.

9. For the history of clerihews and early examples, see E. Clerihew Bentley, *The First Clarihews* (New York: Oxford University Press, 1982).

10. Ibid.

11. John Holt, *How Children Fail* (New York: Pitman, 1964).

12. Roy P. Fairfield, "New Use for the Muse," *Journal of Teacher Education* 20, no. 1 (1969): 17–23. I've quoted only briefly from the article.

13. Ashley Montagu, *Growing Young* (New York: McGraw-Hill, 1981).

14. *Midsummer Night's Dream* 4.2.44ff.

15. See "Art and Its Social Functions" in Ralph Ross and Ernest van den Haag, *The Fabric of Society* (New York: Harcourt Brace & Company, 1957), pp. 333–55. Also see Bob Samples, *The Metaphoric Mind* (Reading, Mass.: Addison-Wesley, 1976) and Sheldon Sacks, ed., *On Metaphor* (Chicago: University of Chicago Press, 1978).

16. Saul Bass, *Why Man Creates* (A Kaiser Film).

17. Michael J. Gelb, *How to Think Like Leonardo Da Vinci* (New York: Delacorte, 1998).

CHAPTER 7

Odd Angles
of Vision

Why "Odd"?/When "Odd"?/
How "Odd"?

There are many definitions of the word "odd"! But the "strange" or "eccentric" seem to fit best here. As suggested elsewhere in this volume, those who create seem "different." They stand out from the crowd. They are frequently "off the scale" or curves of normality, not only by definition but also by their activity. In Western society this is true of artists who live and work in "unreal" or unusual places (usually until they are "successful" or have a patron or institutional sponsor). It is also true of the stereotypical "mad scientist" or "inventor." Even a man like Thomas Edison may have been as well known in his time for his idiosyncrasies as for his inventions; for instance, he was a sleep-cheater, taking frequent naps but rarely sleeping the "normal" eight-hour night.[1]

The "why" question can be answered from many angles. The creative person needs time to himself; otherwise, the world will crowd him so hard or suffocate to the point that he will have little time to sustain the energy it requires to produce a book, a new

---

invention, an embroidery design, a piece of sculpture, a new ballet or opera, a unique football formation, or original corporate configuration. In short, one needs both space and time. This does not deny the brilliant hypothesis occurring in crowded spaces, or even in a dream. It does stress the fact that ordinary, everyday humdrum lives are not likely to produce the great, insightful poem—even though an artist or poet may find his inspiration in such contexts. One poet in south Florida, Campbell McGrath, drew the following headline in the *Miami Herald*: "Poet Mines Everyday Items for Inspiration." Dutch painters in the seventeenth century and American painters in the nineteenth century made history when revolting from "academy-approved" subject matter and standards. Contemporary photographers are enticed by large prizes to catch the moment or candid shot, one that has rarely or never been seen before. Each creator discovers for herself where best to create, in space-time-psyche. But usually away from the "madding crowd," to use Thomas Hardy's well-worn metaphor, hence the claque of photographers who "chase" and sometimes harass celebrities. Twentieth-century poet and novelist May Sarton, in her provocative *Journal of a Solitude*, observes that an author is not totally free to express herself until her parents are dead, and adds that it's important for authors to convert their individual experience into a universal one.[2]

> HEADLINE: a central fact: most people have the occasional flash of insight or vision and can create in that moment *if they but will* and record it for future reflection and action, hopefully, for hundreds or thousands.

This "when" of the individual "flash" is implied by the "why," yet may be approached from at least two angles of vision; namely, (a) the psyche of the creator and (b) the quality of community evaluation.

Every creator, ordinary or famous, must develop enough strength of ego and space-time-motion to "do his thing" when he feels the urge. If this means leaving a social gathering or party at mid-evening to return to his computer to write a poem or another chapter of a book, touch up a painting, add to the score of a new concerto, so be it! If a novelist or dramatist needs to arise at 4 A.M. to work on a scene for a few hours before the household comes alive with hustle-bustle, again, so be it! If an inventor or mathematician solves a problem in a dream or as she's arising, stumbles half asleep through the house or in a hotel room to put *it* down on paper (assuming she doesn't write or sketch in the dark!), she cannot worry too much about the social consequences. In short, the creator's being may be shaped by such spontaneity. That "the world," however defined, may not appreciate or understand such behavior, is probably a "given." If that "world," however, places value in the results of such behavior, then it had best be tolerant if not encouraging. Perhaps those who are concerned about creative endeavors had best build such concern into normative expectations. Those who viewed the film *Amadeus* may recall how quickly the patron-emperor brushed off one of Mozart's compositions when asked what he thought of it. His cryptic response, "too many notes, too many notes." As a product of a society expecting "slow-paced" compositions, Mozart startled him! The tragedy of such offhand judgments, especially where there's power to make them "bite," discourage creativity and the development of human potential. When one listens to congressional critics bash the National Endowment for the Arts, for grants to fund "oddball' projects or ones labeled as "pornographic," one frequently hears evaluations that compare to the emperor's. They are inane and destructive.

And this leads to the "how odd" question—meaning, how strange or eccentric or how far from normal expectations or "community standards"? Naturally, that will depend. With 20/20 hindsight, one may easily see how in the world of painting impressionism led to postimpressionism which led to expressionism and beyond. In fact, it is so easy to trace that evolution with 20/20 hindsight that one wonders how or why critics condemned paintings in that stream of art history. Likewise, with our advantage of knowing about stroboscopic or intermittent light technology, Marcel Duchamp's *Nude Descending the Staircase* seems like a unique way to catch the motion of a human figure as it proceeded down a flight of stairs. But contemporaries, without knowledge of stroboscopic light or cubist potential, might understandably say, "I looked for the nude and for the stairway and saw neither." Perhaps that is one way to approach eccentricity. And no doubt measuring anybody's departure from a norm might take a similar turn. When a contemporary architect seems to defy the laws of gravity, one may easily refer to the Parthenon of classical Greece to observe how its creators used illusion to create similar effects. Note, too, the number of Rube Goldbergs who have attempted to invent a perpetual-motion machine defying laws of physics—although perhaps few had Goldberg's sense of humor! In short, to ask "How odd?" leads to a corollary which is less pejorative; namely, "How unique?"

To answer the question about "uniqueness" requires some knowledge of history of any given field of endeavor. Such clichés as "there's nothing new under the sun" may discourage some would-be creators; it leads to the adage, "Why reinvent the wheel?" On the other hand, in this country there's the other belief (mythology?) about "designing a better mousetrap" or "build a field of dreams and they will come." Also, dreams of getting rich from improving a "gimmick" or "gadget" or "widget" are of legendary proportions.

As significant as Thomas Edison is in the history of American inventions, the day of the single genius-inventor may have been replaced by group research and corporate creators; also, the expense of applying for a patent in this country has become so high that it may discourage "average" persons in assuming the risks involved. And yet, the media focuses so often upon the person who does "make a breakthrough" that the risks may seem worth it. A risk to be calculated. The would-be creator, however, may wish to examine her own motives if she focuses upon uses and wealth rather than the creative impulse and its "natural" consequences. If fear of being different leads a person toward too many sleepless nights, into neurosis or psychosis, then he had best stop to assess relationships between means and ends. If the would-be patent-seeker wants to play probability technically, then he would be well informed to gain the statistics from the U.S. Patent Office before proceeding. Yet, be cautious about scam "artists" who promise too much in the way of greasing the ways to the Patent Office! If the corporate employee discovers that he must sign away the unique inventions or creations that he develops while working for company X, he had best think twice before signing—or employ a lawyer to protect his rights. Hence, the advantage of re-FIRING if possible!

Uniqueness and the Individual

Libraries are full of observations and analyses of the advantages and disadvantages of collectivist versus individualist societies (e.g., the Soviet Union versus the United States). Our derisive (or blind?) attitude toward Soviet creativity before 1957 probably resulted in our collective shock when the Soviets put *Sputnik* into the sky that October. Also, the American Establishment may have been fooled by a biology that demanded conformity to a non-Darwinian set of criteria—or to "art for Marx's sake"—all biological analysis and progress was to prove the superiority of the "New Soviet Man."

Similar differentiation may be found in American society by pitting individualism against community, or even attempting to reconcile those two phenomena in an ever-changing world. Some of the topics and/or queries include:

- How can we talk so much about developing "community" (no matter how defined) while promoting "individualism"? Is it possible to have a "community" of individualists?

- How can we encourage "individuation" or evolution of distinct selves (in the Jungian sense) in the context of focusing upon family values?

- Is it possible to encourage diversity of cultures wherein many of the standards of behavior clash with single sets of values, laws, and a Constitution which presumably are necessary for a "civilized" society?[3]

- Is the two-party political system capable of reconciling simultaneous needs for community and individual efforts and especially the need to create new models of "community" on the one hand and on the other a "level field" for individuals from every gender, race, creed, and clan to create in every field of endeavor?

- Will the economic "religion" of free enterprise and competition accommodate new cooperative modes of enterprise?

- How can the First Church of the Almighty Dollar and the political power that it commands live with other "churches" in a society that is unsophisticated in placing issues and solutions in contexts of paradox and irony?

- And how about the Second Church of Denial serving as a trigger to illusory, delusory, and other pathological perceptions constituting creative processes?

- How long, for instance, can universities tout individualistic achievements and viewpoints while simultaneously raising alumni to be cash cows, and feed said "cows" on rah-rah schemes that include carnival-like, no-brain celebrations that minimize cerebration?

Reared in the Yankee tradition of stubborn, hard-headed, endurance-focused, conservative individualism, I lean toward that emphasis. It is also shaped by my perception that most so-called community *élan* is more mouth music than reality. As a lifelong student of utopian communities that include most of those described by Plato, St. Benedict, Sir Thomas More, Edward Bellamy, Aldous Huxley, B. F. Skinner, and a few contemporary "cults," I find that most fail because of the clash between individuals seeking their own ends and a set of seemingly unachievable community goals. Such goals require a level of cooperative effort that human beings seem resistant to creating and/or sustaining for any appreciable length of time. Ironically enough, cults that end in mass suicide may be the only ones that "succeed." Even mystical political concepts such as Rousseau's *general will* or church communities built around the mythologies of Christ and the Virgin Mary seem to require super organizations, with strong control mechanisms, to "protect" both individualism and community.

While teaching at an emerging, big-time university in the early 1960s, bathing in the clichés and assumptions that "bigger is better" and watching the erosion of most qualitative criteria for determining "best," I wrote a scorching essay, "An Individualist Manifesto."[4] Well aware of the structure of the *Communist Manifesto*, I echoed much of its content, launching my polemic with

> A SPECTER haunts American higher education, the triple-headed specter of conformity, anti-intellectualism, and mediocrity. It haunts the student in classroom, dormitory, sorority, fraternity, and in the thousand natural and unnatural positions he assumes during his four-year campus tenure. It haunts the teacher in the classroom, in his study, and in the many natural and unnatural positions he assumes during a normal academic year. And it no doubt frightens the administrator in his office and in the chambers of his conscience as he watches the thousands of natural and unnatural students pouring onto his campus from every point of the compass.

I move on to explicate this position and provide empirical evidence for it, concluding my *manifesto* with a series of points, much as Karl Marx concluded his. This is a shortened version of that series, both quoting and paraphrasing. In light of my general position in this volume, I encourage readers to apply these viewpoints to your own professional and personal fields of interests, substituting those endeavors for the field of education.

1. We must respect and honor the educational heretic. We need a loyal opposition and especially need acceptance and creation of loyal oppositions.
2. The intellectual life needs models on every campus; honor

students, dean's listers, and Phi Beta Kappa recipients deserve as much support as athletic teams.

3. Every campus should create a committee whose major function would be *never to meet*, have no officers, no minutes, no ritual, no demands except one: it would serve as a model of simplicity, maximum efficiency, and humanity, in short, respect for individual *non*involvement.

4. Assuming the need to institutionalize ideas, courses such as the following should serve as prototypes for every college student in America:

Oneness 101–102—taken as freshmen to promote studying *alone* for at least nine hours/week . . . to counteract tendencies toward togetherness, conformity, anti-intellectualism, and mediocrity.

Silence 201–202—a sophomore sequence to continue the impact of Oneness 101–102, dampen sophomoric (and moronic) boisterousness and egoism and also counteract Lullaby 101–102.

Whyness 301–302—to counteract heady results of mastering coursemanship; develop healthy skepticism about finding "ultimate answers."

Why Whyness 401–402—continues processes begun in Whyness 301–302, preparing learners for commencement and realization that one may have to spend a lifetime assessing factual and theoretical foundations upon which to build job, life, and culture. Some universities may call the course Basic Assumptions Therapy 401–402.

Anti-Senioritis 412—designed especially for those who flunked Whyness or Why Whyness; essentially therapeutic—to cure inflammation of the ego.

5. There is need to construct faculty courses paralleling those for students/learners, to stress importance of counter-organization, counter-busyness, and counter-dogmatic tendencies in university life. Such courses must critique the "publish-or-perish" survival mandate, perhaps reversing the mandate: some publications deserve to perish before printing.

6. Every group should meet immediately to question the basic assumptions upon which they are founded, especially to ask, "How does this group further physical, intellectual, and 'spiritual' growth?"

7. Every board and committee should immediately vote itself out of existence; if that's not practical, then reduce activity by 50 percent to counteract the American propensity to proliferate and join groups—often for the mere sake of joining.

8. Everybody should immediately increase reading and reflection by 25 percent. If necessary, design special programs in Remedial Why Whyness, Trusteemanship, and Advanced Anti-Coursemanship—to say nothing about Idle Curiosity 101–102 for students, 501–502 for faculty.

9. If the above steps are taken, then would-be learners in every context should find time for earnest and in-depth discussion, whether about books, profound social issues, or film versions of same. Once intellectually and humanly alert, students in the wider population may abandon frivolous pursuits for examining Albert Einstein, Arnold Toynbee, and other seminal creators.

10. Every student, professor, administrator, and others engaged in healthy exchange should take an Annual Controversy Proficiency Test to demonstrate awareness of the alternative viewpoints on the key issues of our times.

I conclude my polemic with a view that some of these processes and objectives do exist but warn that "we cannot afford any kind of hypocrisy, individual or institutional. Students, professors, and administrators of America, 'disunite'! The only thing you have to lose is your anonymity." And possibly mendacity!

While nobody has hammered on my door to request rights to publish this essay by the millions or even in a college anthology, I believe that it contains the seeds of ideas related to "community versus individualism." It is my humblest view that many of the creative processes which I advocate in this volume are more likely when individuals cast off the shackles of group-think or "community" dictation than they will to follow the Supreme Court's dictum about "community standards" or the pathological notion of "political correctness." Not a very hopeful prospect, especially at the fringes of "oddness"; yet, that's a risk which the potential creator must run if she's going to take a step forward toward making "unique" contributions. Also, more possible in re-FIREment than the typical retirement.

Social Change and the Quiet Revolution

Recent world history has been filled with "revolution," no matter how one defines it. At the political level, the American and French revolutions have provided models for determining the phases of revolution. Social revolution has been a function of political change and the evolution of technology. Technological revolution has been both slow and swift. Where, for instance, the concept of interchangeable parts has been applied to both material inventions and production processes, we've seen both slow and swift results. The communications revolution, a subrevolutionary force stemming from the technological sector, has accelerated the speed of change from geometric to exponential. These may seem like sweeping generalizations, but there is ample evidence to support them.

But my purpose here is to suggest that *any* would-be creative person has a vast and dynamic arena in which to expand their imaginations, either to promote or impede revolutions. Library shelves are crowded with analyses of formal revolutions, in all their bewildering variety and definition. One seminar that I attended at the University of California at Berkeley at the time of the student-dissent revolution examined more than one hundred different forms. The Russian revolution of four-score-and-more years ago has spawned more books than any one person could expect to read in a lifetime. A simplistic analysis, looking for the justification for such a revolution, will locate ample historical reasons for what happened. A genuine Marxist analysis would, too. And yet, those who focus on the building of the Berlin Wall, what it walled in and walled out, might focus on its dismantling as related to the Cold War. Such are the anomalies of history. In short, one can sketch the big picture. With my own bias toward the acceptance and health of individual achievement, I will continue to emphasize the "revolutions of the mind" and the social contributions that result therefrom. Democratic nations, perhaps by definition, foster social movements that may under most circumstances be perceived as revolutionary. Yet, "true believers" who organize and fuel such revolutions tend to go to extremes, hence the movements do not have wide appeal so in a sense fall by their own dead weight. There is ample literature for those potential creators who wish to "play probability" when debating whether or not to cast their lot for such extreme movements. Of course, the genuine "true believer" is likely to leap anyway, regardless of probabilities. But back to "odd angles."

The Editor as Leveler

No doubt every publication needs an editor, even when a one-person publication is contemplated. Yet, I've often wondered how many creative ideas as well as valuable human expressions and perceptions have been destroyed by editors' inhibitions or single-dimensional grids for evaluation of documents which flow across their desks. Granted, there are libel laws, censorship threats, editorial policies, and other forces that confine texts to rational, legal, and other limits. Yet, having used ample volumes of red ink myself, I can identify with the needs that most editors have to print reasonable materials. But on the other hand I've experienced editors who have been picky-picky, completely out of their depth in a subject-matter field, so biased against a particular intellectual viewpoint and/or expression that they were ill-fitted to deal with a creative idea. Upon one occasion, I battled with a copyeditor for chapter after chapter of a book in order to maintain its integrity. Finally, the copyeditor phoned one day to say that he "couldn't figure out what to do with the last chapter!" By this time I was exasperated, so I blurted, "Had you ever thought of leaving the damned thing alone?" He let the text stand, but the experience conditioned my attitude about "editors as levelers." That is, so many of them don't recognize a fresh idea or have no desire to be associated with it. It's simply "too odd" to see the light of day!

Career as Thing/Object!

Have you ever heard friends or acquaintances talk about the work side of their lives, their "careers" if you will, as though such careers became an *it*, an abstract, separate from living itself, in fact as though the *it* were a *thing*? No doubt many factors in our culture encourage that attitude. Some people's self-concepts virtually coincide with their work-concepts. Ask a woman "who she is" and she may reply "lawyer, teacher, or whatever." Likewise a man may answer "an aviator, machinist, banker." The notion of serving multiple roles is far from a common perception. Early in my working with doctoral learners in the Union Graduate School, I became frustrated when colloquium participants insisted upon driving me into a corner, saw me as a dean or professor, but never both simultaneously. In fact, I attempted to change those perceptions by choosing the title of "coordinator" rather than the traditional "dean" because I figured it was more difficult for anybody to stereotype me if they weren't quite sure what I was doing. At the same time I devised an exercise to use during my self-introductions at colloquia. I asked the participants to close their eyes, then I read a list of twenty-plus roles I had played at various times in my life: son, father, husband, brother, clerk, carpenter, tool coordinator, teacher, camp counselor, etc. To make sure the learners paid attention, I told them that one of my alleged roles on my list was false and asked them to identify it. I varied that item from aviator to sky diver to bank president, etc. Usually, they were accurate in pinpointing the wrong item. But many thanked me for conducting such an exercise and were most cooperative when I turned the tables on them and asked them to mention four or five roles they had "played" in the course of their lives. The net result: it encouraged them to perceive themselves in multiple roles beyond career and begin to think about the possibilities of changing their self-concepts *and* careers. Since I also encouraged them to "follow their dreams" and "fantasies" in the direction of enhancing their learning and expanding their self-concepts, it also reinforced willingness to experiment with a new look at their careers, move them beyond speaking of career in the abstract to experience this role as a function of creative living as well as "making a living."

Exercise No. 15: Who Are *You*?

Perhaps it's time to encourage *you* to delineate the facts and forces that define *you*?

- Do you let your job, housework, or occupation define you? When & Why?

- Make a list of the different roles you take ("play") on any given day (e.g., mother, caregiver, taxi-driver, tutor, etc.) and what is the significance of each? Are there any which you would like to modify? How?

- What fantasies do you have regarding expansion of your roles at home? in your community? in the larger world?

- Wherein do your creations (cooking, singing, toy-making, poems, plays, readings at nursing homes, etc.) define you?

Social Courage and Action

Much has been made of volunteering as a creative mode of re-TIR-ing; it is surely a cornerstone to my concept of re-FIRE-ment. Perhaps there is nothing new to say on the topic *except* to encourage maximizing the experimental approach to reviewing future possibilities. After all, if President Carter's mother could join the Peace Corps at an advanced age, a ninety-four-year-old woman run and complete a road race, or former president George Bush parachute in his seventies, then the sky is the limit, literally! Perhaps the heroes and heroines worthy of emulation are those who live next door and never make the headlines in the local newspaper or on television. In the spirit of Bush's "thousand points of light," but not to duplicate the nauseating publicity about the program, let us encourage inventing new volunteering possibilities. We may be unable to bottle or package human energy, but surely every new artifact or step forward for humanity (on or off the moon!) is a vital part of both a social and an individual legacy. How individuals may wish to be remembered for those legacies will vary from carvings in stone to gardens that mature in a decade. It's just a matter of *doing* then choosing. As one of my former students observed when discussing a sermon he had written: "I called it 'Human Doings' rather than 'Human Beings.'" Or as the Nike logo goes: "Just Do It." Similarly the Star Trek message, "Make it so!"

Short Story as Opportunity

Nothing says that a person cannot embroider his experiences using dozens of different stitches. The following story is very close to an accurate description of a "ragged" landing I once made at the Albuquerque airport . . . *except for the ending*:

> 'Twas a long glide into Albuquerque; yet, we must have danced up and down in the cabin for twice that distance; the captain said *fasten seat belts*; the hostess in the Convair 580 took to the microphone and spoke of "slight turbulence." At one point I looked for the airsick bag and might have used it if a strange movement and new color over the edge of the right wing hadn't attracted my attention.

I looked quickly to see a brown twister dart, zip under our wing and almost simultaneously felt the plane lurch. We soared a bit, plunged. Then, I felt the pilot pull the jet prop into a steep climb and I looked back at a perfect angle to see the twister roar east.

It was scary, but I told myself, "The captain is intelligent and wants to get down in one piece as much as I." In fact I said, "Hail, Captain!" a few times as a kind of mantra under my breath in those split moments of terror.

We leveled, glided, landed, a perfect three-point, beautiful, so smooth. So relieved were the fifty passengers on that Fourth of July flight, we applauded in unison.

I sat calmly, breathed deeply, waited my turn to push down the aisle with my small bag and briefcase. I whispered to myself, "No point in hassling in the aisles to save fifteen seconds." Too, I was determined to shake the captain's hand. They always seem so cut off from passengers. No harm in giving him a pat on the back.

As I came to the cockpit door, the hostess swung it open and I stuck my head in to congratulate the pilot . . . and there to my surprise . . . sitting in the captain's and cocaptain's seats . . . were two chimpanzees.

Anybody with a sense of humor could have written such a "report" or journal entry. The captain on that flight might not have appreciated the levity; yet, the story has a surprise ending primarily because the situation contradicts every expectation of a passenger attempting to reach a destination in one piece. It's simply improbable that a chimp could navigate a plane under such circumstances—though somebody has no doubt tried!

It is my contention that rarely a day passes when some common experience couldn't be stretched via poem, fable, or short story.

Exercise No. 16: Now, Try It!

To sharpen your skills at storytelling and observation as well as a sense of humor, practice writing a short story with a surprise ending! As my old college writing professor advised: get 95 percent of the honey out of the jar quickly because the last 5 percent comes out more slowly!

Of Storytelling

My family was full of storytellers. They carried on the family heritage without too much consciousness or concern of that as a social phenomenon or service. That's how we children (siblings, cousins [even "42nd cousins"], classmates) learned our family histories. That material, too, came mostly through tales about specific individuals. According to my father, my great uncle, Sam, was an itinerant farmworker and tool sharpener, spending a week here and a week there, usually earning his room and board but not much cash. He had the reputation of having poor sanitary habits and table manners. While eating he constantly growled at any food served him: "It's flavored with sawdust." He had a reputation among the farm wives of the country as being an excellent worker but rather a disgruntled person. He was the "poor example" my parents placed before me if I didn't wash properly or didn't care for a particular food. On the other hand, stories told about or by Aunt Eva put her on a pedestal as a desirable role model. My father's mother's stories usually related to the King family, famous in Maine politics. In short, the oral tradition was very much a part of my family life. And the sketches that came to us were more about personal characteristics than events. Both positive and negative role models served the family in teaching values.

My father was a superb storyteller, a master of the timing necessary to use the effective punch line. I think that he and Mark Twain
would have enjoyed one another. Since he ran a small public garage,
he met many a traveling salesman; and, like the proverbial barber-
shop, there was "always" a group of men gathered there telling off-
color stories which "could not be told in polite company." Dad
acknowledged the existence of such stories, but once boasted that he
wouldn't tell any that were not 95 percent humorous. As a boy I listened, learned much about the wayward ways of the world, and developed some of the techniques of storytelling. Hence, I found a contradiction between what Dad said he told as stories and what I heard in
the garage. So at one point, when I developed enough courage to
"speak up," I observed, "Your humor is great, Dad, but your math's
terrible." He laughed but didn't contradict my observation!

No doubt most family life reflects the storytelling tradition
that we find in novels such as Gladys Hasty Carroll's *As the Earth
Turns* or Betty Smith's *A Tree Grows in Brooklyn* or more recent
accounts of Irish immigrants such as Frank McCourt's *Angela's
Ashes*. Such literature is filled with stories, read, absorbed, and
appreciated, generation to generation.

But the oral tradition has been more lively in recent years by
the rebirth of itinerant storytellers and storytelling organizations.
It's safe to say that much of this activity is "big-time." Much of it
is in the tradition of Davy Crockett and Mark Twain. My personal contact with the "movement" comes through one Hugh
Hill, known throughout the network as "Brother Blue." Dressed
in dark blue shirt and slacks, with both butterflies and balloons
added to his costume in great profusion as the years pass, he is a
symbol of the genre as he contorts his Ichabod-Crane-like body
into spectacular and rhythmic gyrations, constantly telling stories
related to his own African American heritage. He speaks from
"soapboxes" in Harvard Square, also TV and radio studios

"around the world," and at storytelling conventions. I met him three decades ago, and encouraged him when he wanted to transfer from the Yale School of Drama to the Union Graduate School to pursue a course of learning that combined dramatic and oral traditions. At our first meeting he showed me the chains that his slave-grandfather once wore. At his graduation meeting, in the Deer Island Prison in Boston Harbor, he demonstrated his learning before a full house of friends, prisoners, TV cameramen, and rumbling prisoners bent on stopping the show and perhaps holding some of us hostage. The police got us out safely—in time to finish his graduation, ironically enough, at the Harvard Faculty Club during one of the most severe thundershowers I ever experienced. Almost every paragraph of Blue's story-filled presentation was punctuated by that flash-bang storm. Today he and his ever-supporting wife, Ruth, are known throughout the storytelling world. I receive postals from them from all over the United States and Europe. He rarely tells a story the same way in two different places. He is a master embroiderer of tales. He and Mark Twain would have made good companions.

I have long claimed that everybody (and I *mean* everybody) has a story to tell *if* there is anybody to listen. It's the task of the storyteller, whether amateur or professional, to develop listeners. This is a creative task in itself. Part of the process involves finding persons who not only like to tell but also listen to stories. The other part is up to the storyteller to find human-interest tales, from family, from friends, from the "human comedy" in which we bathe. Stand-up comedy or U.S. and Brit-coms may provide sets of role models, but Einstein talking over the back fence as he exchanges lollipops with children for help with their arithmetic and my own exchanging of haiku with teenagers may afford better examples. Likewise, developing a sensitivity to the human hunger for vignettes about family, neighbors, and even famous people is another route for gathering rich materials for storytelling.

Exercise No. 17: Never to Forget!

1. Recall a vivid story from your family tradition, from your own schooling and peers, from any source with focus on "vivid," a story you'll never forget!
2. Recall a story that you've heard so often you might like to forget it! Does repetition strengthen the tradition or weaken it? Why?
3. Do you possess a few stories that you might caption: "My Stories"? Try committing them to paper.
4. Try "translating" any of the above stories from the oral to the written mode of expression. What's the difference between "getting yourself over the footlights" to writing a story which doesn't depend upon presence of the author?
5. Develop a written statement (a journal entry?) about your learning from this exercise.

To distinguish between illusion that is corruptive, and illusion that may be a foundation for imagination: Ah, there's the rub! It's not all that easy to distinguish virtual reality that is the foundation for so many of today's television commercials and the imagination it may require a scientist to conceive as "brilliant hypothesis" to solve a scientific problem. While I do not argue any of these issues technically, any layperson can make the application to everyday life.

Notes

1. See the children's book *The Value of Creativity: The Story of Thomas Edison*, by Ann Donigan Johnson (La Jolla, Calif.: Value Communications, 1981).

2. May Sarton, *Journal of Solitude* (New York: W. W. Norton, 1973).

3. Barbara Okun, Jane Fried, and Marcia L. Okun, *Understanding Diversity: A Learning-as-Practice Primer* (Pacific Grove: Brooks/Cole, 1999).

4. Roy P. Fairfield, "An Individualist Manifesto," *Phi Delta Kappan* (February 1964): 230–35.

CHAPTER 8

Illusion: Friend, Enemy, or Both?

Illusion comes in many styles and faces. And 'tis no wonder. From Plato's time in the fifth century B.C.E. to the twentieth-century's Michael Polanyi, the nature of illusion has been an enduring question. If, as Plato claimed, the only reality is the realm of ideas, then logically enough, the physical world is all illusion. Surely those who remember his famous "Allegory of the Cave" will recall his dramatic illustrations of the shadows on the cave wall. On the other hand, Polanyi and his spiritual followers lean in the other direction; personal knowledge, however real to the person, could be an illusion and the only reality for that person. It could be a delusion. The story of teaching and learning, belief and proof, during the past 2,500 years is one of the great pieces of drama that constitutes the educational, philosophical, theological, and scientific streams of world history. It seems safe to predict that the tension between these perspectives may be a key issue of the twenty-first century.

One needs only to reflect for a moment to appreciate the extent of technological "advances" in the past century to understand galloping illusion (followers in the Platonic tradition might call it "deception"). Painters since the Renaissance have utilized illusion as a fundamental structural problem, hence the use of aerial and linear perspective to overcome two-dimensional limitations of materials they've used. The work of the impressionists and expressionists continued the trend, only to be outdone by those in evolving film techniques, until it is not surprising to hear Woody Allen claim that his "intellect is all an illusion."[1] And, of course the "solid" particles comprising an ordinary object have been pretty much shattered by modern physics. All of which leads to "virtual reality" as the essence of illusion. But let us go back a "few years" or so to appreciate the extent of technological advances.

Only two decades ago, a CBS report on advertising revealed that the average citizen was exposed to five thousand ads per day, 3 percent of which were "remembered" and more than 90 percent "wasted." Today, we are bombarded by similar statistics, many of them related to violence on TV and how to curb it or minimize its impact. Looking toward fundamentals: anybody familiar with the fine arts in the twentieth century is well aware of the insight that Saul Bass made in his film *Why Man Creates*; namely, that art is "looking at one thing and seeing another."[2] M. C. Escher, the Dutch etcher and probably the finest illusionist prior to the "virtual realists," enabled us to see water running uphill and soldiers walking down the up staircase. Those who saw the popular film *Never on Sunday* may recall the hero, Homer, trying to explain theatrical death to the prostitute he was attempting to reform. But she was not fooled by the "dying" actors and actresses; she saw them taking their bows at the end of each play and knew that they "all went to the seashore" in their real lives. Today's "legitimate" theaters can be technologized to the nth degree in order to create illusions comparable to those used in film's virtual reality. One further illustration: the cartoon character Ziggy recently approached his dinner table to say, "It was only a matter of time . . . my alphabet soup is spelling out little advertisements." Ironically enough, in our ultramaterialistic world, illusion is a prime method for immersing us in images that may lead us to buy, buy, buy!

In short, the technological and communications revolutions have realized what Marshall McLuhan, the Canadian communications expert, observed about "massaging" the "messages," or: the "medium is the message."[3] And living in a sensate culture as we do, we are frequently victims of both outer and inner illusions. My own propensity toward writing doggerel/grooks led to an interchange with a colleague who was everlastingly remarking, "Give us this day, our daily illusion." I responded, "You opt for order/I'll take confusion!" It was a good-natured exchange.

Now, confusion may not be so "bad" as long as one is aware of the challenges that lack of order or chaos presents. Paralleling the English poet's view of spring following winter with delightful inevitability, I'm tempted to observe, "When illusion dominates, can disillusion be far behind?" In looking at the history of teaching, preaching, and parental guidance, surely warnings against being taken in by the "illusionists" is understandable, especially when those guiding the learning or even indoctrination were certain that material focus was corrupting values. This is a complex matter, not to be solved by simple generalizations.

Solutions? If the commercial and political "spin doctors" have their way about it, we will probably continue to bathe in the sea of illusory images. After all, it's part of the liturgy of the First Church of the Almighty Dollar and Second Church of Denial. *Mis*information and *Dis*information are already official governmental policies as any student of comparative government will attest. But there are counterforces such as regulatory agencies. Private groups—national, state, and local—battle the trends; yet, it's difficult to fight the power of official Washington, Hollywood, or Madison Avenue, especially when encountering the money to be made and the seduction of TV. Yet, we probably have not reached the saturation point. Illusion may become even more dominant before we experience both massive and healthy social reaction. We may have to get sicker before we get "weller"! Possibly consumer groups as well as specialized Paul Reveres will continue their warnings about the financial illusions and scams which ruin those taken in. Many women have learned to identify "the glass ceilings" and develop tactics and strategies for getting through them. The field is wide open for evolving a million ways to *use* illusion both positively and negatively.

Typical Americans would probably advocate that we develop some kind of "pill" or gimmick, such as 3-D glasses, to clear our vision. Or perhaps some entrepreneur could develop a line of products that would include illusion shields, illusion scramblers, and illusion transformers comparable to the chip fixes which parents may now use to block out "undesirable" TV programs for their children. Ironically, such products might become the basis for multimillion-dollar industries and save citizens from the "work" they might have to expend to protect themselves from being "taken"—all of which would convey their message . . . via TV! And it is important, too, to observe that the sense of sight is not the only one wherein illusion takes over and where thoughtful analysis and common sense leave off. For instance, note the impact that contemporary popular music and the classical minimalists have had in "fooling the ears." The fast-food industry and the gourmet cook have one thing in common: "Fool the tongue!" The senses of touch and smell have similar "enemies" or "friends," as one prefers. And surely we know enough about magic, ESP, religious cults, and other efforts to stimulate the five senses, as well as the phenomenon of intuition, to know that research and education in this area will no doubt keep an army of statisticians and professors busy for the next several generations.

Exercise No. 18: Emulating Leonardo

- Consult Michael Gelb's *How to Think Like Leonardo Da Vinci: Seven Steps to Genius Every Day*; see especially part 2, "The Seven Da Vincian Principles." Try his exercises for sharpening curiosity, testing knowledge, and refining senses. Assess your progress in developing some of da Vinci's abilities. (You don't have to be a genius to improve your senses; perhaps one step at a time will prove to be satisfying and lead to creations you never dreamed of.)

- Just as you may have sharpened your ability to distinguish colors via writing haiku, perhaps you can gain from "do-it-yourself" drawing by turning to part 3 of Gelb's book.

- Invent your own tests for double-checking your senses via Gelb's suggestions. At first be generous, utilizing your own home or familiar surroundings; then, as subtly as you need to be, carry the tests into unfamiliar places, a park or mall or office building. Do you notice any differences between the two types of location? What are they and how can you sharpen both?

For all of the exercises in this volume and consideration of the place illusion may have in our lives, it seems to me that we are left with some central questions; namely, can we slow the rate at which corruptive illusion dominates our lives? And if we're successful, how will that free us to be creative with more time and options available free from illusion's clutches? Or will technology continue its bulldozing ways to govern our thinking, our buying, our opinions, our very dreaming? Are regulating agencies using humanistic or economic criteria for making operating policies, and what difference does it make? Do educators at any level dare revise their curriculums so that Illusion 101–102 may reach parity with Math, History, or Economics 101–102? Will you as a citizen of the Twenty-first Century become any more sophisticated in "seeing through" money-grubbing scams or the mumbo-jumbo of authoritarian ideologies than residents of other civilizations and centuries? How can people of the next century reverse the manufacture of guilt, perhaps the most insidious product of most religious history, guilt that profits TV evangelicals, credit-card purchasing, get-rich quick schemes, and other illusory activity?

Illusion, Rhetoric, and Disillusion?

Questions to ponder and discuss:

> And what about the framework of our own illusions for organizing our experience? Could we maintain our sanity without it?

> Is there a "truth" to something Carl Jung allegedly claimed; namely, that 95 percent of all perception is psychological projection? Is the percentage too high or too low?

> To what extent and with what consequence do we construct our private mythologies (*I* am honest; *they* are the enemy!) to reinforce the cultural, illusion-supported myths under which we live ("Democracy and capitalism are good." "The president has power.").

> Can we have a clear sense of our own personal identities if we will not admit to fostering illusions; projecting our

values to our seeing and hearing, to our total Being; perpetuating obsolescent mythologies and/or creating new ones to the point (almost?) of extending the self-fulfilling prophecy into the self-deceiving one?

With what consequence do we ignore the insights of linguists and semanticists that the language we use conditions perception (of illusions and/or disillusions) whether that language be the English of common usage, Americanese, the jargon of our particular field of endeavor, slang and/or newly invented words, or second languages from around the world?

If dreams, fantasies, and metaphors serve as images projected onto our reality screens, as found theater, wherein does this test our coping?

AND: When rhetoric appears, can illusion be far behind?

So let's wrap it up by examining human legacies. Hopefully this consideration will suggest ways to examine your own, also by including a Do-It-Yourself Re-FIRE-ment Kit that may encourage you to bend over, as Henry David Thoreau suggested any of us might do, to look at aging from an upside-down position.

Notes

1. *Miami Herald,* January 24, 1997.
2. Saul Bass, *Why Man Creates* (A Kaiser Film).
3. Marshall McLuhan, *Understanding Media* (New York: Dutton, 1966).

E P I L O G U E

Count UP to Inspire

When Jim Owens, author of the doctoral manuscript listed in the bibliography, learned that I was doing a book on creativity, he sent me an e-mail letter, which read, in part, "I hope . . . there is a chapter on fear, pain, and terror—I have been so in touch with all of those; especially with the wildlife, skunks, and snakes." He had just been "living in isolation in San Acacio [Colorado], renovating, reading, sleeping and writing. The place has a mystical energy for rest and recuperation and creating being. I have reorganized my life and checkbook, and marvel at the output."[1]

Well, I didn't write such a chapter, but what Jim was talking about is certainly implicit in much that I have said. Surely, as psychologist Rollo May says in his book *The Courage to Create,* and educator Parker Palmer in his volume *The Courage to Teach*, a person may not only encounter ecstasy when having a "bright idea," a new angle of vision, and other emotions discussed here, but also fears that may result from others' judgments, from being "written off," from being given "unfair" treatment, and from being neglected. But there is one constant that any teacher serving primarily as a facilitator of learning and/or creativity can count on: motivating people to contribute to both social and personal legacies.

One of my former colleagues, Dorothea Leonard, a professor of psychology in Miami, discussing notions about "living legacies" which elders or others might create, assembled them in categories:[2]

Creative Works—paintings, sewing, woodwork, writings of all kinds

Past History—stories, traditions, rituals, religious experiences

Genetic Endowment—physical diseases and health of ancestors

Family Trees—one's lineage, struggles, victories as well as defeats

Myths—generational repetitions of irrational and rational messages

Talents and Interests—music, athletics, dramatics, culinary arts

Patterns that continue to recur, both positive and negative

With such a grid before her, no teacher, preacher, or other leader in a position to exert influence (no matter the uncertainty of causality) should lack for a motive to move her "students" into a creative vogue. Before attempting such motivation, such a "teacher" may wish to engage in a discussion of some of the following questions about legacy as related to creative urges.

It might begin with consideration of that classic query: "Does the tree falling in the forest make any noise if there's nobody around to hear the crash?" Then the discussion could move on with some of the following questions:

1. How must a legacy be formulated to make itself manifest?
2. Must it or they be documented or documentable?
3. If a person feels or thinks that he has little or no legacy, does that diminish him, or should it change his self-concept?
4. Need a person necessarily "invent" a philosophy of being to call it a legacy (e.g., M. K. Gandhi's "satyagraha" or Smith's Mormonism)?

5. How should we distinguish between a legacy and a résumé?
6. What about other questions or angles of vision?

Before discussing this topic at one seminar, I found it helpful to analyze the way in which I followed family patterns, reversed them radically, or merely modified them.[3] On the one hand, I chose to study more or less intangible family characteristics/values such as honesty; generosity; kindly yet judgmental; spiritual or nonmaterial; individualistic; loyalty to friends, family, and institutions; and religious. On the other hand I chose what I called external patterns such as unreconstructed Republicanism, slogan-mongering, storytelling, practicality, education, intellectual behavior, use of hands, community service, and work ethic. Such an analysis was also helpful in determining which of my own creative urges was original and which merely copycat. Writing a few poems about the phenomenon also helped clarify. One, for instance, was entitled "Legacies: Tangential or Tangible":

> Must you
> touch it
> shape it
> make it tangible
> for all to see
>   your legacy
> or maybe
> freeze your smile
> walk another mile
>   in ecstasy?

Another: "Legacies to Ponder . . .":

His was a legacy
of generosity
could never say "No!"
if asked "to do . . ."
gave away hours
as though eternity
were his to give
always in conflict
with "unjust powers"
yet battles
carefully picked . . .

In the second and concluding part of this epilogue, I shall stand one of my do-it-yourself kits on its head, Count Down to Re-FIRE-ment. Meanwhile, I would suggest that creativity and legacy discussions afford any facilitator of learning or changer of behavior patterns the opportunity to dream up and count up ways to inspire.

A Do-It-Yourself
Re-FIRE-ment Kit

10. Begin to dream up thoughts and words to evoke images which will counter the usual ones; instead of "retirement," why not "aspirement" or better still "re-FIRE-ment"? Instead of images such as nursing homes, wrinkles, crippling diseases, why not concoct images which open up the world, such as energy, mountains, flowing waters, vast seas, or snowscapes?

9. Begin to list projects you've been wanting to do, ones you *really want to do*, not ones that guilt or other paralytic

forces told you that you must do. If it's a matter of cleaning the cellar because it's "dirty" or "messy," forget about it! If it's gone that long, it surely can wait another twenty years. As discussed in "Zen and Housekeeping" in chapter 5, "If it's not worth doing, it's not worth doing well!"

8. Think of at least two or three activities which will afford some sense of continuity from work life to the retired (re-FIRED) phase of your being. If you like to read, why not continue with reading? If you've enjoyed playing golf, bridge, or horseshoes, then keep swinging; if sex has been central, then give *it* "the old college try" and "go-go-go"! The same would apply to whittling, needlework, stopping at the bar on a rainy night, volunteer nursing, and so on. In short, focus on maintaining momentum.

7. On the money scene: begin to disregard cost-of-living indices; they'll scare the hell out of you every time, and tell you that your money will be worth only half as much in five to seven years. If you're planning to move to Israel, Russia, or Brazil, you'll probably halve your purchasing power in a single year (of course, that shock treatment could be beneficial and save the agony of "creeping inflation"!). More practically:

   a) chances are 9 to 1 that you'll not consume in the same mode, hence the indices may be irrelevant or at worst, quasi-irrelevant;

   b) chances are, your common sense will be better than the sense (cents?) of those economists who presume to advise the American people.

   c) furthermore, you'll have more time to study costs of commodities and avoid the ones that rise fastest.

6. Practice constant irreverence toward clichés about retirement, cost of living, senility, etc. Develop a well-orches-

trated blasphemy regarding any event/word/expression normally associated with being crippled, products to improve denture sticking, boredom, etc. By taking an irreverent stance, this virtually guarantees nonapathy. Better than aspirin, Tylenol, and painkillers by other names. Perhaps such attitudes will carry over into the constant flow of images related to politicians, sports heroes, and those next-door neighbors who insist upon cluttering up your spaces with noise, nonsensical small talk, and irritations about constipation and precipitation.

    a) An important corollary: talk back to commentators dispensing the evening news; consider if watching the news is good or bad for your health. Try checking your blood pressure before and after watching for an evening or four.

5. This attitude, as above, may also help reduce fuel bills! As Michelangelo is alleged to have responded while painting the Sistine Chapel and asked about being cold, "Indignation keeps me warm!" (in Italian of course!). You can adjust your body thermostat in accord with your blood pressure.

4. Space requirements: You may need more or you may need less living space, depending upon habit and transitional lifestyles; but now is the time to begin perceiving space from new angles of vision, maybe asking:

    a) How much does my family need? What don't we need? What is comfortable and what is merely convenient?

    b) How can we "carve" out spaces relevant to visitors, offspring, neighbors, old friends and new, the folk from Washington and Mars (is there a difference)?

    c) How can we make a tighter integration of space, time, and psyche or psychological need (what I call "space-time-psyche")?

Since a person cannot avoid being in space, in time, and in one's own mind simultaneously, then seeing those forces in a kind of gestalt (or whole) will not only make relating to the world easier but also clearer. You know where-how-when you stand. And perhaps you could relate to my view of health; namely, free-floating in space-time-psyche, free of the normal restrictions of job, "three-score-and-ten," and societal definitions of sanity and infirmity.

3. If you have not recently calculated your Laughter Quotient (LQ), then find a "funny" friend who will "level" with you to help you determine what that quotient is. If need be, make your own list of criteria by which to test your LQ, day to day, year by year, decade by decade. In short, what kind of cartoons, TV sit-coms, jokes, films, and short stories make you laugh? Also do *you* make you laugh? After all, isn't it you who wants to laugh more without feeling sad or guilty about it? Or do you? You may eventually agree with me that laughter could be our *last best cope* against the idiocies of everyday life. As a preparation for extremes coming to extremes, familiarize yourself with Norman Cousins's *Anatomy of an Illness* where he discusses laughter (especially in viewing Marx Brothers, W. C. Fields, and Joe E. Brown films) as one aspect of nursing himself back to health after a near-lethal poisoning.

2. Learn more about your metabolism and how to feel healthier without being sick about it. Swallow a little Zen instead of capsules! There's nothing neurotic about feeling good about being good; nor does one have to feel bad about feeling good despite the guilt factories of the world. Also, if you've made your peace with the universe, maybe you'll not *feel* perverse about *being* perverse by all normal standards. For instance, if God is really "god" to you, then

swearing is probably okay. Ditto atheism, joking about reformed druids or other out-of-orbit viewpoints! Also you may feel more open about criticizing Americans who worship in the First Church of the Almighty Dollar or those who cripple themselves by joining the Second Church of Denial. And so much of "feeling better" or wellness is "going with the flow" and/or "not pushing the river."

1. If none of these steps seems to work and you do not share the vision of aging as a freeing, creative, and re-FIRING process (with both individual and social implications), then forget retirement. Keep working until you drop in your habitual tracks. If you follow the proverbial route and "work yourself to death," you'll never have to worry about facing this life transition. You'll also be spared of facing your creative potential!

Notes

1. Quoted with permission.

2. Dorothea Leonard, handout at a Miami Discussion Group, 1995.

3. Richard Stone, *Stories, The Family Legacy: A Guide for Recollection and Sharing* (The Story Work Institute Press, P.O. Box 941551, Maitland, MD; 1994). A helpful, illustrated guidebook for ways in which to preserve family legacy; the table of contents alone is worth the cost of the forty-page pamphlet.

Working Bibliography

There are libraries full of materials on the topic of creativity, and also museums, art galleries, and science and technology exhibits that demonstrate it. Every fair, be it a world's or state or county or even a city sidewalk festival, offers opportunity for anybody to delve deeply into the human urges to create, whether space rocket, a new seed, or "wild" art display. Hence, I'm entitling this "Working Bibliography," and keeping it short in the hope that persons reading it may move beyond the references in the notes at the end of each chapter and explore other materials with a discovery mood and mode.

Bachelard, Gaston. *The Poetics of Space*. Boston: Beacon, 1969.
———. *The Poetics of Reverie: Childhood, Language and the Cosmos*. Boston: Beacon, 1971.
Briggs, John, *Fire in the Crucible: The Alchemy of Creative Genius*. New York: St. Martin's Press, 1988.
Cameron, Julia. *The Artist's Way: A Spiritual Path to Higher Creativity*. New York: Tarcher/Putnam, 1992.
Dixon, Edla. *Antioch: The Dixon Era, 1959–1975*. Saco, Maine: Bastille Books, 1991.

Fairfield, Roy P., ed. *Humanistic Frontiers in American Education.* Englewood Cliffs, N.J.: Prentice-Hall, 1971.

———, ed. *Humanizing the Workplace.* Amherst, N.Y.: Prometheus Books, 1974.

———. *Person-Centered Graduate Education.* Amherst, N.Y.: Prometheus Books, 1977.

———, ed. *The Federalist Papers.* 2d ed. Baltimore: Johns Hopkins University Press, 1981.

———. *New Compass Points.* Saco, Maine: Bastille Books, 1988.

———. *Angles of Vision.* Saco, Maine: Bastille Books, 1993.

———. *Seaside Fables and Other Incites.* Saco, Maine: Bastille Books, 1994.

Gach, Gary. *Writers.Net: Every Writer's Essential Guide to Online Resources and Opportunities.* Rocklin, Calif.: Prima Pub., 1997.

Hershman, D. Jablow, and Julian Lieb. *The Key to Genius: Manic-Depression and the Creative Life.* Amherst, N.Y.: Prometheus Books, 1988.

Hirsch, Edward, ed. *Vision: Writers on Art.* Boston: Little, Brown, 1994.

May, Rollo. *The Courage to Create.* New York: W. W. Norton, 1975.

Osborn, Alex, *Applied Imagination: Principles and Procedures of Creative Problem-Solving.* 3d ed. New York: Scribner, 1963.

Owens, James. *Artists of Time: Myth, Metaphor and Making a Living.* Ph.D. diss., Capella University, 1998.

Richards, Mary Caroline. *Centering in Pottery, Poetry, and the Person.* Middletown, Conn.: Wesleyan University Press, 1969.

Romey, William. *Consciousness and Creativity: Transcending Science, Humanities, and the Arts.* Canton, N.Y.: Ash Lad Press, 1975.

Sewell, Elizabeth. *The Orphic Voice: Poetry and Natural History.* New York: Harper-Torchbook, 1971.

Teacher, Janet Bukovinsky, and Jenny Powell. *Women of Words: A*

Personal Introduction to Thirty-Five Important Writers. Philadelphia: Courage Books, 1994.

Waldrop, Stanley. *Closeness and Creativity: A Collection of Lectures, Responses, and a Final Exam.* Mt. Baldy, Calif.: Waldrop Publications, 1970.

World Institute. "Methodology of the Creative Process, Contributors Issue." *Fields Within Fields . . . Within Fields* 2, no. 1 (1969).

———. "The Methodology of Pattern." *Fields Within Fields . . . Within Fields* 5, no. 1 (1972).

Index